Adelaide Cioni
On Patterns

Mousse Publishing

Foreword

by
Daria Khan

March 8: International Women's Day, and the opening of Adelaide Cioni's exhibition *Ab Ovo / On Patterns* at Mimosa House. The symbolism of this intersection is not coincidental. Mimosa House, founded in 2017 with a mission to support women and queer artists, adopted its name from the mimosa plant, embracing its activist, medicinal and mythological potentialities and narratives. The mimosa was chosen by Italian feminists after the Second World War as a symbol for International Women's Day, because this spontaneous, robust and bright yellow plant was accessible to all during the spring season in Italy. It reproduces itself through powdery lumps, which stain clothes, and leave its powder on our hands. Its persistent yellow pollen is a reminder of the resistance and courage of women who have been fighting for our freedoms, and whose achievements haven't been fully acknowledged.

Adelaide Cioni once wrote: "The problem with feminism is the same as the problem with painting flowers. Just as you cannot not be feminist you cannot not paint flowers." Geometrical shapes, deriving from flowers, plants, and body parts are at the basis of Cioni's visual language. The artist's hand-painted canvases and fabrics feature repeated monochromatic dots, circles, triangles, zig zags, that act as proto-signs of a universal language that immerses us in a primordial world. Cioni's patterns are affective: they hold a softness and delicacy, reminiscent of old faded wallpapers and fabrics that absorbed memories and touches of people who painted, embroidered, and wore them throughout centuries.

The after-images of these patterns keep vibrating on our retina after we leave the exhibition space—they proliferate to infinity, beyond the borders of canvases, signalling the insistence and continuity of memory, of narrative, and of presence.

Cioni's work carries feminist undertones in every painterly and performative gesture, as the artist points out:

> "to be feminist means to defend that part of you which has a different voice, another syntax, another way of imagining the world. To be a woman, in a world that has been shaped and told by men, means to be an outsider, a presence which is ultimately incomprehensible, and which is in constant need of a translation."

In this solo exhibition *Ab Ovo*—"from the egg," her first in the UK, Cioni revisits the very beginning of nature and creation, providing Mimosa House with a significant occasion to reassert our core values as they are manifested with affection and empathy in Cioni's work.

Casting a Spell: Adelaide Cioni's Patterns

by
Jennifer Higgie

I'm at Adelaide Cioni's studio in Hackney Wick. It's freezing cold and grey outside but her small room is an oasis of colour and warmth. On the wall are three large, vivid paintings on unstretched cloth: green-blue repetitions of a wave-like motif that undulates like a series of moustaches in the air, a group of pale red crosses, and a choppy composition of bright yellow beak-like shapes. Colours are simplified, forms distilled: these are modest, hypnotic images that throb with life. The artist makes tea and tells me she's been working on her pattern project for three years. As we talk, she returns to her fascination with artforms that have "no verbal aspect":[1] devoid of narrative, they create their own language, atmosphere and meaning as they tap into something at once very old and very new.

What is it about pattern that is so enduring? Adelaide talks with amazement about the fact that many of the geometric shapes we see in modern art and contemporary design are not only present in ancient, and even prehistoric art ("we were dressed in skins and were drawing triangles!"), but in nature too: in plants. Patterns have been around for millennia, in paintings, the decorative arts and—especially—in weavings, many of which were, and are, traditionally made by women. It seems

1 Unless otherwise mentioned, all quotes from Jennifer Higgie studio visit with Adelaide Cioni, London, 10 February 2023.

relevant here to mention that in Sanskrit *tantra* means "loom," "weave," and "treatise," and that both "textile" and "text" are derived from the Latin *texere*, or "to weave." While the meaning of an image or a pattern is never precise (no art ever is) their resonance is profound: the meaning splinters, rearranges, and weaves its way through imaginations. "I wonder: How can a pattern be reassuring? Why do they comfort us or please the eye? Is it their intimation of infinity, like the sea?" A central question preoccupies Adelaide. She explains: "Narration is a way to tame time. You create an arc, a story, and you can understand it. But when you go beyond narration, perhaps you're stepping beyond time—you're accessing another dimension. . . . If you talk to me for hours but don't tell me a story what are you telling me? What is beyond story telling?"

Her answer to her question is multifaceted but it strikes me that, in their bold simplicity, Adelaide's paintings reverberate in space like mantras. Repetition is both the imposition of order on chaos and an invitation to explore altered states. Prayers often

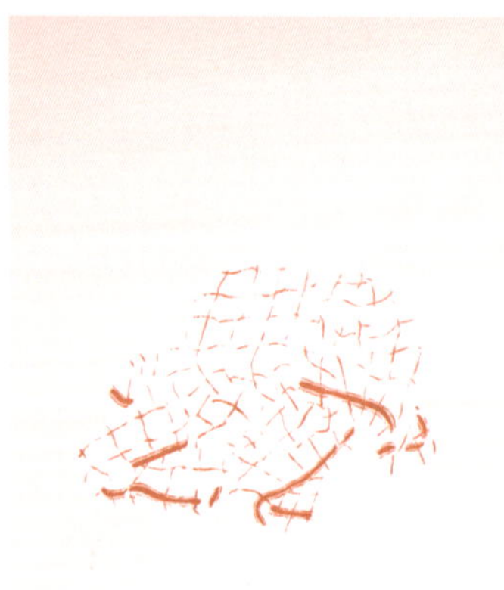

Adelaide Cioni, *Esercizi di traduzione*, 2017, vinyl paint on paper, 46 × 34 cm

involve the repetition of a word or phrase, and music across the globe employs repeated sonic motifs to heighten emotional engagement. Adelaide writes to me about this melding of body and mind:

> "The heart, our internal organs are repetitive and constant. They are the bass line of our existence. And patterns are a portrayal of the bass line of our existence. You can play on top of them, you can even hide them, but they're there."[2]

Apart from her two invented patterns—the waves and the beaks—Adelaide's recent patterns were inspired by visits to archaeological digs across Italy. Reframing quotations is a way, she feels, of plugging into memories that have been collectively shared across place, time and medium. Repetition, here, is not a degrading of the original but the renewal of cosmic truths.

"Secondary images"—acrylic paint sketches, drawings, and wool stitched on canvas—are studies of elements of a painting that are peripheral to a central image. Adelaide explains: "You might be looking at a painting of Apollo and Daphne, and you're thinking about their story, but meanwhile, your brain is recording the sea, the way the leaves are portrayed; a checkerboard, a golden column, black holes,

2 Adelaide Cioni, "The line crosses space," sent to Jennifer Higgie, 14 February 2023.

the sun." She's fascinated by the fact that a still life is more than the sum of its parts; how the overlooked objects that we use every day can contain worlds. For a while she was fixated on tape; she loves its curves and angles and how, in most households, it's both ubiquitous and invisible. Adelaide is an animist: she has long felt that objects have a unique power or energy. She says: "I look at an apple and I enter it." When she's feeling down, she likes to focus on birdsong and flowers. She writes: "Everything is subject to change on this planet, even rocks. Everything is alive. Even corpses. Everything breathes and radiates energy of some kind."[3]

For ten years, Adelaide was a translator of American literature and it inflects her work as an artist —after all, artists, too, are translators of an idea or an influence. I ask her what prompted her to change course. She replied: "Translators are a vessel for someone else's creativity. I wanted to do something for me." In 2015, she began an ongoing series titled *Translation Exercises: Viaggio in Svizzera* (2015)—continuing her interest in commonplace objects—a painting of a green striped tea towel against a monochrome, flesh-coloured background, and yet it could also be a study in colour and line. Her work often mines the border between abstraction and figuration: "Where" she asks, "does a ra-

3 Adelaide Cioni, "The line crosses space," sent to Jennifer Higgie, 14 February 2023.

diator simply become a series of lines? . . . What happens between the original and my translation, why are translations always different and why do I prefer one to another?" In a similar vein, her recent series *Bello o più bello (Beautiful or More Beautiful)* (2022) comprises four screen-printed drawings of bold, simplified shapes—a circle, and a wonky bean- or worm-like shape—in primary colours, accompanied by brief texts: Italian translations of English phrases such as "Beautiful or more beautiful," "Before or after," "Kant or Heidegger," and "Long or very long." The tension between the image and the words is both playful and dreamlike: intuitive, surprising, fresh. These are pictures that make clear that art, like translation, is not a precise science. Adelaide writes to me:

> "It's funny how all these words have to do with space: translate from *translare*, or to take to the other side, and approximate from *approssimare*, to go close. It's all about moving in relation to a centre core, on the two sides of it, or

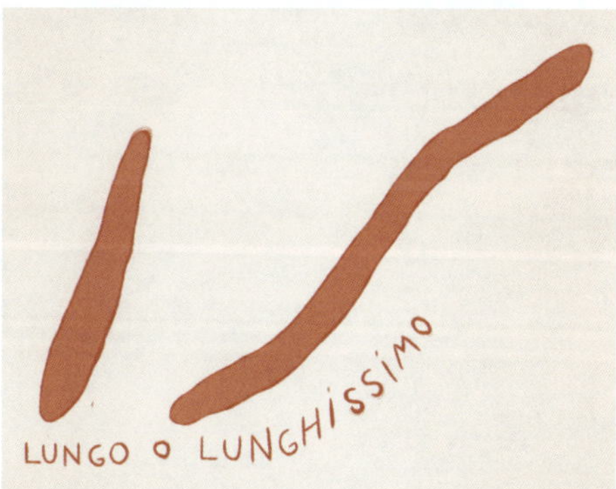

Adelaide Cioni, *Lungo o Lunghissimo*, 2022, vinyl paint and Indian ink on canvas, 155 × 200 cm

close to it, but apparently we're rarely able to be completely and exactly 'in it,' even though we constantly try to get there."[4]

As an artist, Adelaide believes it's important to work on yourself, "your vulnerability, your way of being in the world." She's intent on stripping back the ego and seeing what lies beyond it, "in the soul or spirit." She says: "For art to do what I want to the ego shouldn't be there." An artist whose practice is "always about drawing," marks—or what Adelaide calls "signs," a response to what she describes as an object's "vibrations"—a response to the melding of the body and the mind in the act of creation. When she was translating texts, she says she tended to "forget her body," and that of the writer whose work she was transforming. After a while, she wondered: "Where was John Cheever's body when he was writing? How did that impact on the words he chose? And why should we assume that it's the mind making decisions? . . . I imagine my knee choosing a word." She feels that words are very strange; although they're immaterial, "they have to pass through our bodies, our bodies filter them." This applies to drawing, too. I ask her why it's so important to think of our earthly containers when making a work of art.

4 Email from Adelaide Cioni to Jennifer Higgie, 11 February 2023.

She replies that:

> "If we remember we are bodies we become better people. Bodies feel pain. To understand that other people are equally vulnerable creates empathy. In the end we are all bodies that have to deal with other bodies. It's easier to let go of the ego if we remain aware of our bodies."

I ask her what the word "spirit" means to her. She pauses and says: "It's the inside force, like breath, it's something you don't see but it keeps everything alive. The drawing is the closest thing we have to the trace of the spirit." She recalls a quote by Bridget Riley, who sees the act of painting as one of translating "a text unknown even to yourself," which demands the ability to "learn to listen, because it is through a special kind of listening, a sort of 'listening in,' that one learns how to speak."[5] Later, she sends me a short piece she has written. It's called "The Line Crosses Space" and includes the observation: "When the pencil leaves its mark on the paper or canvas or wall, I'm casting a spell. I am uttering a prayer. Make it happen. Make me whole with the cosmos."[6]

5 Bridget Riley, "Painting Now," 1996, in *The Eye's Mind: Bridget Riley, Collected writings 1965–1999*, ed. Robert Kudielka (London: Thames & Hudson, 1999), 211.

6 Adelaide Cioni, "The Line Crosses Space," sent to Jennifer Higgie, 14 February 2023.

Adelaide has titled her new body of work *Songs* because she sees patterns as a way of visualising rhythm in space. In her studio, she shows me a selection of works, painted on various fabrics, from 1930s hand-spun linen to lighter calicos; they'll be hung from the ceiling in the gallery, like banners, moving gently as the air and visitors circulate. For the opening of her forthcoming exhibition *Ab Ovo*—which translates as "from the egg, from the very beginning"—dancers, in costumes designed by Adelaide, will weave their way among the textile works, moving to a commissioned piece of music.

Back home, I open a file from *Songs* on my laptop. There are more than seventy of them: rough, red triangles and crosses, floating across a pale ground, like marks scratched into stone walls; thick black lines, like tyre marks in snow; hot red triangles, dense with colour, cropped at their edges, like a glimpse of flags on a hilltop; indigo circles, sap-green leaf shapes and more. They're so simple, they're complex. I think of something that Adelaide wrote:

> "Making/drawing a pattern is like singing a song. Projecting out your own rhythm, your own vibration. To see it double itself, to have confirmation of your being real. To affirm your presence. To say yes. Yes I am."[7]

7 Adelaide Cioni, "The Line Crosses Space," sent to Jennifer Higgie, 14 February 2023.

References:

Riley, Bridget, "Painting Now," 1996, in *The Eye's Mind: Bridget Riley, Collected Writings 1965–1999*, ed. Robert Kudielka. London: Thames & Hudson, 1999.

Dancing on Patterns

by
Ilaria Puri Purini

It is a cold evening in 2022. An audience gathers in a private house in west London for a performance by Adelaide Cioni. The living room has been transformed into a theatre set, draped in white cloth daubed with large black triangles. Seated on the floor, musician Dom Bouffard begins to layer elegiac lines of guitar into reverberating slices of sound, and then a figure appears wearing a white and red costume. The cloth she wears envelopes her body. Dancer Typhaine Delaup would be unrecognisable in the cloth and its great red circular stripes, were it not for her fierce face—the only part of her that is visible aside from her bare feet. Wooden poles attached to the lower part of the cape elongate Delaup's arms. To a sound of shimmering menace, she stretches, swirls, and swings the costume to create patterns of ephemeral lines, circles, half-moons, and points. Suddenly, this Catherine wheel performance ends as it began, as a superimposition of signs, music and dance that reaches a crescendo, ebbs, and ends.

Cioni's visual vocabulary stems from geometric motifs: points, squares, rectangles, chevrons, and stripes. In *Prayers to Jupiter* (2022) the dancer adds arm movements and these create new figures, particularly circles and semi-circles. In time and with speed, the covered body disappears leaving just the visual impact of the movement simultaneously dancing and drawing. Between these disciplines are familiar thresholds that delineate art practice and media: abstraction and figuration, material and immaterial. We find a creative tension that has provoked theses of art practice and theses of art history, as it did for Wassily Kandinsky who recalled watching the dancer Gret Palucca at the Bauhaus in the 1920s: "What is she doing? Dancing or drawing?" Kandinsky included photographs and drawings of Palucca's geometrical shaped dances in *Point and Line to Plane* (1926), his influential textbook presented to his Bauhaus students.[1] Kandinsky was dealing with the effects of the impersonality of abstraction when expressed by the physicality of the body. He used basic geometrical forms—point, line, and plane—to respond to dancers like Palucca, to answer the questions that she moved in him. Palucca was testing the potential of abstraction of her body, pushing the boundaries of abstraction into her own physicality. Not specifically interested in drawing, Palucca was interested in how a circle, a square, a triangle might dance. Her own physical quest for abstraction provoked questions amongst her male counterparts.

Cioni's dialogue with certain aspects of modernism also navigates a series of questions coordinated

1 Wassily Kandinsky, *Point and Line to Plane* (New York: Dover Publications, 2012), 26.

by a kind of geometry: "a point where drawing can go into the three dimensions, but not in stone, not in iron, not in bronze. It's not sculpture, it's space." The fusion of body and space is achieved by the invisible marks produced by the dancer while moving. In the performance *Prayers to Jupiter* the dancer, the music, and the setting are simultaneously bringing about a point in space, while also acknowledging a power beyond the body, the intervals between dancing and drawing. The marks of the body are not yet tangible, they are visible as they disappear. As dancing, drawing has a privileged relation with the body, sharing physicality, temporality, and a way of thinking that is immediate and wordless. All these elements are fundamental to Adelaide Cioni's practice. They relate to a non-narrative, abstract approach, made of patterns and motifs.

Prayers to Jupiter has echoes of the French American dancer Loïe Fuller, who in the early 1900s contributed to the genesis of a choreographed abstraction. Using a thin robe which she would manipulate through elongated poles in her hands, Fuller

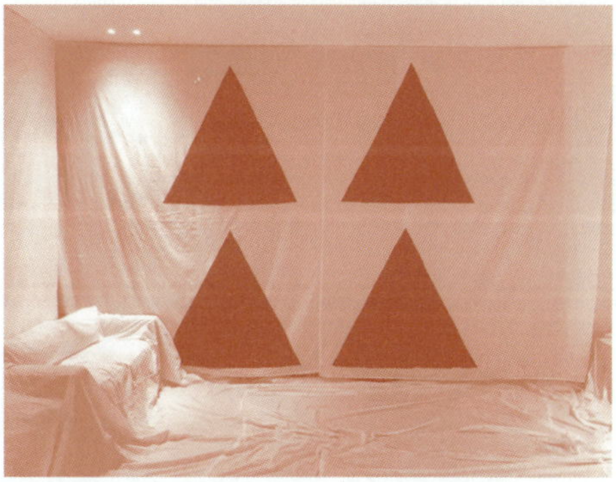

Set for *Prayers to Jupiter*, 2022.

created patterns and figures in space. She maximised the use of light, sound and movement, and her Futurist contemporaries considered her an emblematic reference in their search for simultaneity.
It was a synthesis of different elements and a form of kinetics that proved attractive. Cioni's quest for abstraction rhymes with efforts to create a synesthetic experience where sight, sound and rhythm are empathetically shared with audiences. This then places a demand of attention on audiences, such that they too, confronted with non-narrativity, may question what she is doing—dancing or drawing or something else.

Adelaide Cioni has traced her interest in costumes to 2016, when she assisted costume designer Greta Goiris, who was collaborating with William Kentridge on the performance associated with his mural *Triumphs and Laments* (2016) in Rome:

> "Dressing the performers for the show, working with the costumes, I experienced something

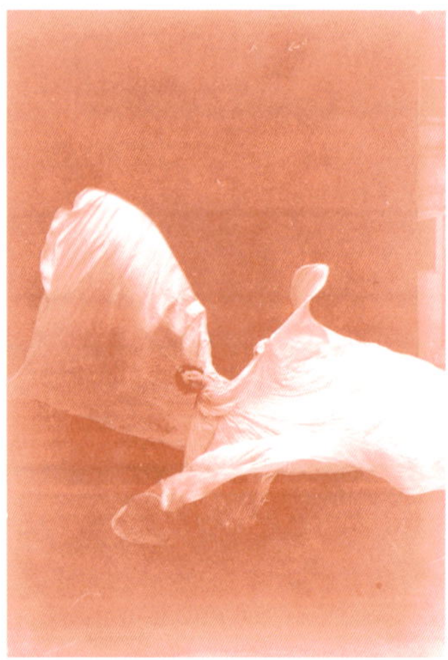

Isaiah West Taber, *Loïe Fuller in La danse Blanche*, 1897.

> which would stay with me ever after. It was a work of care and play with the performers, very intimate, and joyful, like preparing them to go to war, except it wasn't war but a huge game, and it gave me the idea and the feeling of the relationship that we can establish with a piece of fabric. How the simple fact of wearing a particular dress allows us to enter a ritualistic state, and feel stronger, able, connected."

Adelaide's interest in the body connects with practices of rituals, magic and the acquisition of empathy; she found in clothing a simple act of care and metamorphosis.

In keeping with a sensitivity to and a care for human bodies, their changing and situational qualities, Adelaide Cioni has performed in her costumes on different occasions.[2] In contrast to Fuller's costumes, hers are made using heavy cottons. Sometimes she uses old, reused antique fabrics gathered over the years. These she cuts and folds into garments with knife-edge pleats that follow a body's different motions. Like other simple garments—capes, drapes, and togas—they loosely cover and animate, disguising and transforming those that wear them, and those that, in turn, they remake. In this vein, Cioni describes her costumes as "large draw-

2 Adelaide Cioni has performed in *Il rimosso* with Fabio Giorgi Alberti, Suzzara Art Prize, 2016; in *Pink Punk Performance* with Fabio Giorgi Alberti, in the exhibition *Da Franco, Senza Appuntamento*, curated by Vasco Forconi and Andrea Polichetti, 2017; and in *Capes and Modules*, studio performance, 2020.

ings that one can wear." The costumes force the body back upon a physicality of movement but also into an uncanny presence of a body that has undergone depersonalisation. Visual pleasure is found stripped of the erotic engagements that tend to confine bodies. And so, despite their labours, audiences view a greater plurality of meaning and sensation.

Tactility is important to Cioni's practice, as Agnieszka Gratza mentions in her essay in this catalogue. For the exhibition *Ab Ovo / On Patterns* at Mimosa House in 2023, Cioni conceived an experiential walk through her work. The paintings/textiles in the entrance prepare visitors and familiarise them with the performance that takes place in the following space. The paintings on old linen are made of large black triangles, small-scale green patterns that evoke the sea, small-scale black dots, red diagonals, bright yellow cylinders, orange triangles. The viewer must pass through and amongst them, touch their coarseness and smell their atmosphere. Her preferred palette is made of bold red, black, yellow, green, and blue. All of these colourful marks and their spontaneity trace an irregularity and repetition of pattern, emphasising a human touch even where it has departed. Cioni is not sentimental, the paintings are to be viewed and valued as objects with many uses: "at any moment fabric can be folded up." The ephemerality of linen and cloth, gendered work—repeated, arduous—makes for art to be folded up and to remake another place, whether gallery or home.

The costumes of Cioni can be compared to Hélio Oiticica's *parangolés*—the wearable, colourful, asymmetrical garments initiated in 1964. Oiticica asked friends to enter the museum in Rio wearing the cloak-like robes during a retrospective. These friends, mostly coming from the *favelas* of Rio, wore the costumes while shaking and dancing, an impromptu parade to break the staid seriousness of the occasion. The *parangolés* confronted the museum's criteria for what is considered art, and the racial and class tensions that surround institutional power. In Cioni's work the political aspect finds a collective voice in care, in the craft of clothing dancers, and in the uniform materiality of costume that breaks out into action.

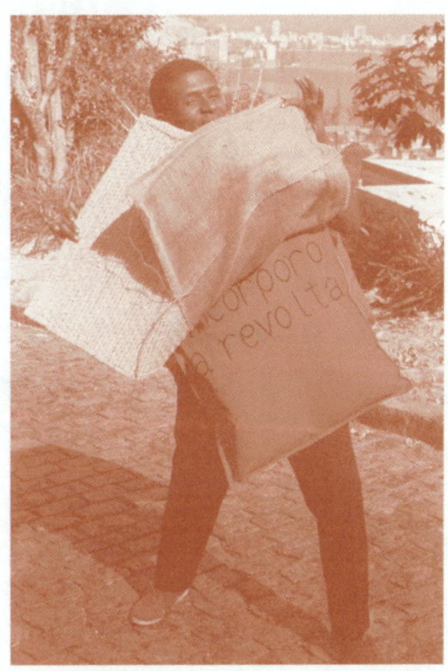

Nildo of Mangueira wearing *Parangolé P15 Cape 11 – "Incorporo a revolta,"* 1967 © César and Claudio Oiticica. Photography by Claudio Oiticica.

Cioni's paintings and costumes are displayed for her new performance *Song for a Square, a Circle, a Triangle* (2023), exhibited at Mimosa House. Here they have a unique relationship with the decorative mural. Before being hung on display, the costumes are worn by the dancers, in the centre of the room. Each dancer wears a different costume that covers their body and focuses the attention on the abstractness of each design. As in *Prayers to Jupiter*, the back wall is also covered by a large black and white pattern. The body becomes matter–neither female nor masculine but a fluid rhythm that resonates with the rest of the patterns—"a play without parts or plots" that seeks to symbolically inhabit the dynamics of personal, collective, and political movement.

The patterns are visual, musical, physical, and also embodied through a primordial root within ourselves. The triangles on the walls and the lines in the costume emphasise musical rhythms. Cioni has often worked in collaboration with writers, dancers, and musicians, and she refers to this collaborative way of working as an important way to explore a practice that traverses multiple platforms. She constructs abstract pictorial representations that transform spatial contexts into flat, ornamental compositions. As Penelope Curtis writes there is "surface tension, held in a complex balance, negative and positive."[3] Similarly, the patterns created by Cioni explore the dichotomies of abstraction. These oscillate between color/whiteness and empty/full giving a rhythmic understanding to her compositions. The gridded works are interwoven with concentric circles, and patterns seem to play rhythmically, this often gives a joyful and light element to her displays. It also intimately connects the body and the space, creating a heightened awareness in the viewer. The extension of the style and aesthetic of one medium, multiplies into others. The decorative becomes the stuff of the pictorial, and the pictorial, decorative.

3 Penelope Curtis, *The Pliable Plane, The Wall as Surface in Sculpture and Architecture, 1945–75* (London: Mack Books, 2022), 102.

References:
Curtis, Penelope, *The Pliable Plane, The Wall as Surface in Sculpture and Architecture, 1945–75*. London: Mack Books, 2022.
Kandinsky, Wassily, *Point and Line to Plane*. New York: Dover Publications, 2012.

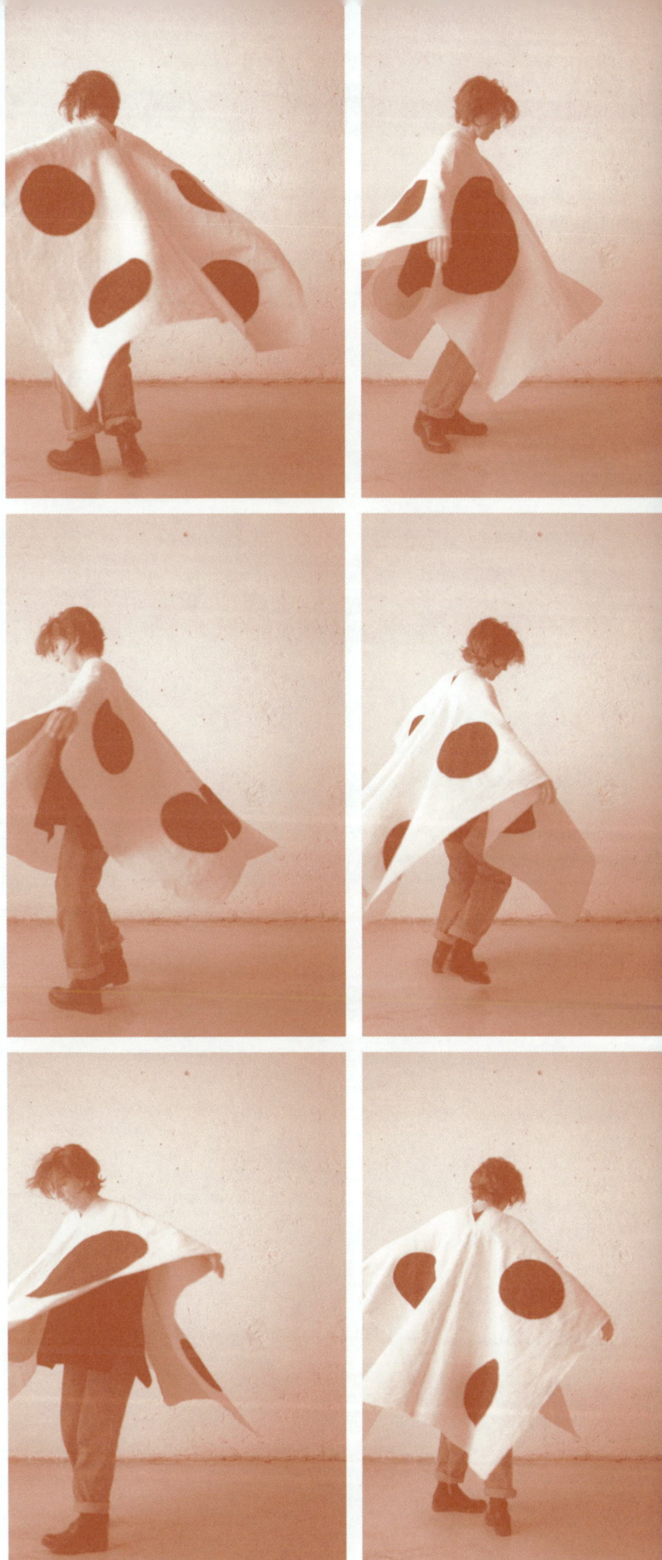

Adelaide Cioni, *Cape*, 2020, costume, wool stitched on hemp fabric

Adelaide Cioni: Geometry, Repetition, Action

by
Jareh Das

Decorative patterns are found in every culture across the world and also in nature. Patterns can be both cultural and natural—they can represent heritage and sociopolitics in a visual form, and can be found in the natural world as part of our everyday environment. Patterns in global cultures are part of everyday life whether found in the vernacular of architecture, craft objects (textiles, pottery, metalwork) and even on bodies in the form of scarification and tattoos. They have strong metaphorical and cultural meanings, alongside cosmological dimensions connected to ancestry. Whether their origins are African, Mayan, Islamic, European, or Aztec, patterns are universal and move beyond borders, where recognisable symbols recur and become evident. In the Islamic decorative canon, for example, dominated by calligraphy, surface decorations such as the arabesque are based on rhythmic linear patterns. Scrolling and interlacing foliage and plain lines are often combined with other elements and usually consist of a single design which can be "tiled" or seamlessly repeated as many times as desired. Geometric laws are followed, rather than naturally obtained.

African textiles, on the other hand, are as diverse as the myriad of ethnic groups across the continent. From Kente found in Ghana to Manjak in the Gambia and Senegal, elaborately designed handwoven textiles with decorative patterns continue to function as a means of communication, information, and mutual association within particular communities. There is spiritual and historical significance, and the symbols used, often directly relate to historical proverbs and events. These patterns represent a form of storytelling in place of written language to convey messages of importance for an individual, family, or larger social unit. What is evident in surveying the global use of decorative patterns is a rootedness in symbolism and repetition to convey meaning as a way of passing on ancestry, major historical events, beliefs, legends, and other cultural elements in cultures where orality takes precedence over written language. Modern and contemporary artists turned to patterns for regularity and rhythm in their work; Ellsworth Kelly, Sol LeWitt, Piet Mondrian and notably, Yayoi Kusama, who has used repetition as a form of therapy to calm anxiety and depression, celebrating what she describes as a generous unpretentiousness to the recurring motifs in her works.

The starting point of any pattern is the single element that will be repeated. This is called a motif. Adelaide Cioni's use of decorative patterns centres on motifs and her artistic practice resonates on the one hand with how patterns have historically conveyed meaning beyond written language across cultures. On the other hand, the artist moves beyond the narrative function of patterns in her performances, paintings, drawings, and films and instead posits them as material explorations that allow limitless possibilities beyond language. Cioni attends to the repetition and multiplicities of the way motifs become an unspoken form of communication that vibrates and pulsates across canvas surfaces, screens, and wearable objects. Nature is the central grounding framework for the artist's works with its seemingly perfect formations of pattern adorning bark and leaves, that appear symmetrical from a distance. On closer examination they reveal their imperfections, as wonky, broken lines, a beauty and poetry of the incomplete yet one that is always in flux.

Cioni also cites a range of influences from which she draws inspiration, including Hawaiian kapa textiles. Another inspiration is minimalist painter Agnes Martin whose deeply meditative and compulsive studies in lines, bands, patterned grids, and colour reflect on order and tranquillity expanding across surfaces suggestive of wide-open spaces. Martin was fascinated by the prospect of art as the visual representation of a mystical, otherworldly realm, but was informed by nature and, like Kusama, turned to art as an escape from her mental health struggles. She wrote:

> "nature is like parting a curtain, you go into it. I want to draw a certain response like this . . . that quality of response from people when they leave themselves behind, often experienced in nature, an experience of simple joy . . . My paintings are about merging, about formlessness . . . A world without objects, without interruption."[1]

In 1966, the exhibition *Systemic Painting* featuring twenty-eight artists including Jo Baer, Larry Poons, David Novros, and Agnes Martin was organised by the influential art critic Lawrence Alloway who coined the phrase which gave the show its title. It was a way to describe a field of increasingly popular geometric abstract paintings and artworks with a simple, methodical, organisation exploring repetition and pattern.[2] Cioni takes this much further and is more expansive in her approach using repetition and action to approach the geometry of abstract patterns. Patterns are for the artist the visualisation of a rhythm in space, "the bass line of our existence," as Cioni states, repetitive and constant in every aspect of our lives.

1 Olivia Laing, "Agnes Martin: the artist mystic who disappeared into the desert," *The Guardian Art and Design* 222 (May 2015), https://www.theguardian.com/artanddesign/2015/may/22/agnes-martin-the-artist-mystic-who-disappeared-into-the-desert.

2 See Lawrence Alloway, *Systemic Painting* (New York: Solomon R. Guggenheim Foundation, 1966).

Kew. A Conversation in Green (2019), is a Super8 silent film by the artist who captures the symmetrical surfaces of palm trees, flowers, and other vegetation showing variances in the colour green, textures, and leaf formations; it was shot in the Palm House in Kew Gardens, London. This film gives an insight into Cioni's astute observation of and deep engagement with nature: the natural geometry of plants with their lateral veins outstretched, lines merging to form leaves that sway poetically and respond to changes in the environment, but in other instances are still. It is this essence of nature that Cioni conveys in both the film and resulting monochromatic (or "schematic" drawings, as the artist refers to them) which make up her series *Palms* (2019). Black ink and green brushstrokes on a white background hold in time the movements of palm fronds, swaying or still, depending on the image conjured in the mind when viewing these drawings. The American poet Emily Dickinson comes to mind as she saw nature as something intrinsic that can never fully be known due to man's limited imagination. On nature, Dickinson writes: "To pity those that know her not/ Is helped by the regret/ That those who know her, know her less/ The nearer her they get."[3] Nature's mysticism has no limit as it is a baffling force that defies all analysis. In the film

3 "What mystery pervades a well!" by Emily Dickinson, Emily Dickinson Collection Repository, Amherst College Archives & Special Collections, (Box 6 Folder 55), access and use online, https://acdc.amherst.edu/view/asc:12993.

Kew. A Conversation in Green Cioni is attempting not to analyse but simply to capture the complexities of nature's infinitum.

Across drawings, paintings, stitched canvases, installations, and performances featuring wearable textiles Cioni depicts recurring motifs including triangles (*Drawings for Myself. Red Triangles*, 2020), circles (*Ab Ovo. Five Red Circles*, 2020), squares (*Drawings for Myself. Red Squares*, 2020), and grids (*Grid for My Friend the Anarchist*, 2020) in a variety of colours. In what might be described as a compulsive journey into studies of the symbols she encountered on travels, in texts, and visits to museums, these motifs span a timeline from the prehistoric to the present, again speaking of their universality and recurrence, but more importantly, their existence outside of time. This is made evident in her multifaceted *Ab Ovo* series (from the Latin meaning literally "from the egg," this phrase

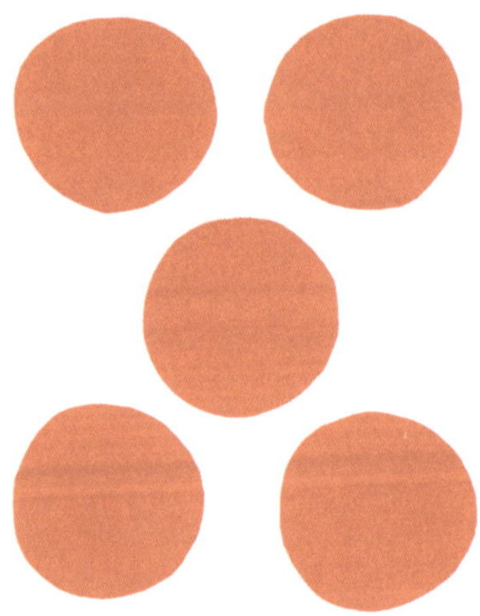

Adelaide Cioni, *Ab Ovo. Five Red Circles*, 2020, fabric stitched on canvas, 103 × 82 cm

is used to suggest “from the very beginning”). *Ab Ovo* is, according to the artist, “an investigation on the recurrence of certain decorations, from prehistory to the Renaissance to the present, and it springs to some extent from an interest in language: these images narrate nothing, there are no protagonists, no story, no words of reference or symbols to decipher.”[4]

In a recent performance, *Prayers to Jupiter* (2022) with dancers Typhaine Delaup and musician Dom Bouffard, Cioni’s spiral motif animates a cloak-like robe brought to life by the performer through movement, negotiating space and the weightiness of the fabric itself. The two-dimensional becomes sculptural and even architectural, moving into the performative, yet, once the event ceases, textiles return to being static, inanimate, folded to be packed and stored away. For the current exhibition *Ab Ovo / On Patterns*, Cioni has painted handwoven fabrics

4 Adelaide Cioni, exh. cat. P420, Bologna (2019), 32.

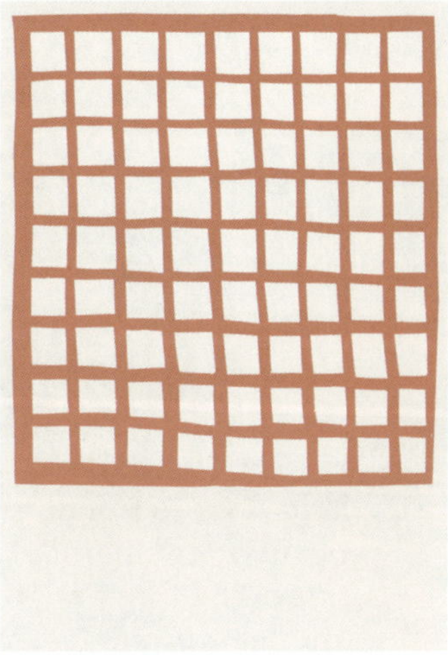

Adelaide Cioni, *Grid for My Friend the Anarchist*, 2020, paper collage, 102 × 72 cm

gifted to the artist and originating from Tuscany. These fabrics were once used as dowry for marriage rites and are transformed into wearable cloaks which make up an installation to be activated through performance, enlivened by the body to show how music and the dancing body respond to these abstract patterns. When not activated, there is an invitation to touch and perhaps imagine being adorned in them.[5] "Why fabric? Why not paint? There is something more to fabric, it is in space and related to the body in a different way than paint," Cioni has explained. Her preference is to take a non-narrative approach dealing with materiality and action in her process of making.

5 Cioni explained that some of the handwoven fabrics were made in Tuscany in the 1930s and were given to her by a friend whose grandparents owned land close to Barga. The fabrics were woven by farmers and used as part of the dowry of their daughters, to make sheets, tablecloths, towels, and curtains. The farmers grew hemp alongside other crops. The hemp was spun and then woven on small looms with a 65/70 cm width.

References:

Alloway, Lawrence, *Systemic Painting*, New York: Solomon R. Guggenheim Foundation, 1966.

Dickinson, Emily, "What mystery pervades a well!," Emily Dickinson Collection Repository, Amherst College Archives & Special Collections, Box 6 Folder 55, access and use online, https://acdc.amherst.edu/view/asc:12993.

Laing, Olivia, "Agnes Martin: the artist mystic who disappeared into the desert," *The Guardian Art and Design* 222 (May 2015).

All About Palms (of the Green and Pink Variety)

by
Agnieszka Gratza

"Palmes...!
Alors on te baignait dans l'eau-de-feuilles-vertes;
et l'eau encore était du soleil vert"
Saint-John Perse, "Pour fêter une enfance," *Éloges* (1911).[1]

The first work by Adelaide Cioni I ever laid eyes on was *Ab Ovo. Green palm* (2020), which was mounted on the concrete wall of Villa Lontana's garage-turned-temporary exhibition space in an outlying area of Rome. It stood out from the other artworks brought together for the *Painting Stone* exhibition at Villa Lontana in 2021 through its stark biomorphic motif, plain yet assertive. Upon closer inspection, what I took to be a painted figure against a neutral off-white ground turned out to be a single piece of dark green-blue woolen fabric painstakingly stitched onto canvas. It had a rich texture that seemingly grew out of the cloth surface, one that positively invited touch.

The "green palm" bore little resemblance to its counterpart in nature and the way it is usually depicted. If anything, it was a palm leaf—not straightforwardly of either the fan-shaped or feathery variety, yet combining attributes of both. The squat green shape recalled ancient ivory or wooden combs with irregular teeth, or else blades of grass. The negative space of the canvas around it made me think of

1 Author's translation: "Palms . . . ! / Back then they bathed you in green-leaf-water; and the water was still green sun," from Saint-John Perse, "Pour fêter une enfance," *Éloges* (Paris: Gallimard, 1948/1911).

stalactites growing down from a cave's ceiling and, inevitably, of fingers, even though the seven-pronged "palm" ruled out any obvious comparisons with the human hand. In English—but the same holds true of Latin and other Indo-European languages—the palm tree is so named for its visual affinity with the palm of an outspread hand. In his ode to childhood, the prose poem "To Celebrate a Childhood" based on memories of growing up in Guadeloupe, the French poet and diplomat Saint-John Perse repeatedly invokes palms and associates the tree with tactile sensations and images of hands.

The curious palm motif, as I later learned from the artist, is in fact sourced from a ninth-century glazed plate of Iraqi origin found in the V&A collections. It is spaced around the rim of a whiteware dish at regular intervals, corresponding to the four cardinal points, its vivid green hue contrasting with a more elaborate but somewhat faded blue-tinged pattern reminiscent of a pine branch. "Its decoration combines green splashes with plant-based designs painted in blue," the label reads. We can safely assume that the motif Cioni picked out corresponds to the

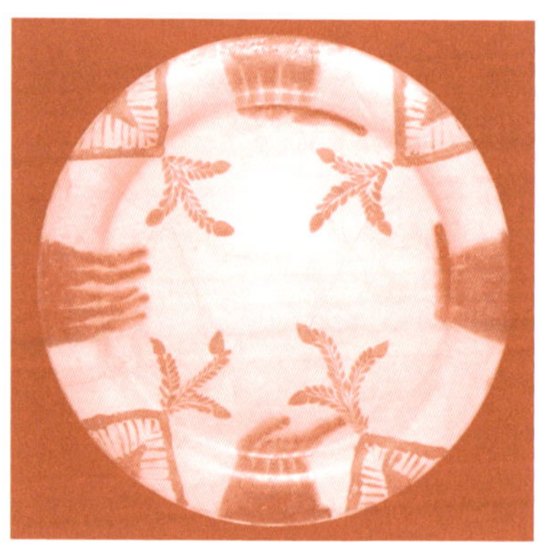

Decorated whiteware dish, Iraq, probably Basra, 850-950, V&A Collections (Museum no. C65-1934)

"green splashes" in the V&A description; nowhere does it mention a palm. That Cioni should see it as a "palm bent down in the wind" has more to tell us about the way fantasy operates than about the motif itself.[2]

In *Fantasia* (1977), published in the year that he conducted his "tactile workshops" for children at the Pinacoteca di Brera in Milan, the Italian designer and artist Bruno Munari sets out to explore the creative processes that lead to the birth of an idea or the making of an artwork, partly so as to demystify them. What we owe to fantasy can but need not be absolutely new, for instance, as is the case with Cioni's "green palm" which appropriates an existing decorative pattern. Fantasy, according to Munari, hinges precisely on the ability to make relations between the things we know, and the more it has to play with, the more active it is. Adults often attribute this faculty to children, Munari claims, when all they really do is project what they know onto what they are less familiar with. Hence the need to expose children from an early age to the greatest variety of objects and games that appeal to different senses, above all that of touch, in order to stimulate their creativity.

2 In a conversation with the author, 3 December 2022.

At Villa Lontana, Cioni's *Ab Ovo. Green Palm* (2020), had a companion piece: a short film shot with a Super8 camera inside the Palm House at Kew Gardens. Projected in a recessed space diagonally across from where the sewn painting was displayed, *Kew. A Conversation in Green* (2019), was also in dialogue with *Ab Ovo. Green Palm*, no doubt informing my interpretation of their subject-matter. While the woven dull surface of the stitched fabric appeared to absorb light, the film projected out into the surrounding space a radiant greenness that drew the eye. From up close, both the fixed and the moving image had a fuzzy, almost velvety appearance. In the case of *Kew. A Conversation in Green*, this has to do with the choice of the analogue film, whose grainy quality beautifully conveys the depth and gradients of the green mentioned in the subtitle as well as the varied textures of the tropical plants. Watching the film as the camera lingers on the crisp fan-like folds of palm fronds, the ribbed patterns of a banana leaf, or the spiky edges of a succulent plant whose polished surface has a metallic sheen, is also a tactile experience.

The film bears witness to an intimate acquaintance with the inhabitants of the Palm House, an architectural wonder and a glasshouse of an unprecedented size at the time when it was built in 1844, anticipating the Crystal Palace. In January 2019, Cioni spent a month living nearby with her partner, and she found comfort in the warm and tepid atmosphere of the glasshouse, ideally suited for tropical plants, not just palms. "Inside the Palm House I felt at home, among very interesting friends," she confided.[3] She would film and draw in there for hours, and the resulting *Palms* drawings and film capture the peculiarities and whimsical ways of the different plants and their companion species. The hand-held camera imparts motion to sessile leaves and branches in the film and a sense of movement softens the otherwise daunting architectonics of plant anatomy drawn live in *Palms*.

A symphony in green, Cioni's only filmic work is practically but not quite a monochrome. Halfway into the three-minute film, a robin with a russet breast and throat makes a fleeting appearance, and then, towards the very end, the camera zooms in and scans a phallic red inflorescence sheaved in the delicate red spathe of an arum lily plant, seemingly erect. "When we begin to question the world our first dialogue is with nature. Flowers are the arousal of nature," writes Cioni in a manifesto of sorts that sets the tone for the publication *And the Flowers Too* accompanying the exhibition of that name that she curated for the Fondazione VOLUME! in the autumn

3 In an email exchange with the author, 25 January 2022.

of 2021. Flowers are indeed the plants' reproductive organs and their beauty, from an evolutionary point of view, is but a means of ensuring sexual selection.

Staged amid plants in the glasshouses of the Botanical Garden of Rome, boasting a fine collection of outdoor palm trees, the group show included Cioni's own works grappling with a tricky theme to which artists return again and again. Visual excerpts from a larger prize-winning installation, *À propos de bacchelli 5* (2014), her etchings made on photographic film of hot pink cyclamens that filled the woods surrounding the house she grew up in Bologna, were projected onto a white screen using a Kodak slide carousel. What is the problem with painting flowers then? To quote from Cioni's text, which yielded the exhibition's title, "in the end we all want to paint the sense of sex. And the flowers too."

Self-Portrait With a Red Hand (2017), the first of the artist's works exploring the human body, is in some ways the most overtly sexual one. Nearly square in format, it resembles a contact sheet with rows of neatly aligned vignettes—4 x 5 inches—each picturing a pair of white thighs outlined in black ink with a hint of pubic hair at the point where they meet. As one reads the storyboard from left to right and top to bottom, the red hand gradually comes into the picture, slowly edging towards the triangle even as the thighs spread further, by degrees, until the red fingers reach their goal and latch onto it. Made in the same year, *Neofeminism*, is more graphic still: a furry, evocatively shaped black island floats on a sea of pink in this fabric work.

A more muted shade of fleshy pink wool is used to suggest human skin in the *To Be Naked* (2020) sewn painting series. As with the *Ab ovo* works, which features a mix of geometric and organic forms drawn from nature (besides the "green palm" and the sister "green leaf" and "green algae," there are thunderbolts, stars, wave patterns, and of course the eponymous egg), the body parts singled out with each new work in *To Be Naked* are invariably presented against an off-white canvas backdrop. Although the artist does not dye the wool herself, she sews the cut outs to the canvas by hand, using a plain stitch. For Cioni, the appeal of working with fabric, as opposed to paint, which is all plane and abstraction, has to do with its materiality. The fabric strikes her as being a body in its own right, with a texture, a thickness and a weight to it. The stitch is a boundary line in this respect, signalling the point where the two bodies—that of the cut out and that of the canvas—touch.

Two of the works in the *To Be Naked* series were included in the *Io dico io – I say I* group exhibition at Rome's Galleria Nazionale d'Arte Moderna (GNAM) in 2021, where I got to see them. Appropriately for a show marked by a feminist outlook, starting with its title borrowed from critic Carla Lonzi's autobiographical writings, these two works dealt with the two most eroticised parts of a female body, breasts and legs respectively. The visual impact of *To Be Naked. Breasts* (2020) in the show was particularly strong, owing to where it was displayed: you could see the work at the end of a sequence of communicating gallery rooms, framed by a set of receding door openings. Rather than a frontal, flattened out view of breasts—something that Cioni has experimented with elsewhere[4]—here we are presented with their cross-section: two mounds, each crowned by a miniature version of the main rounded shape in red, standing for the nipple. This last detail calls to mind Agnes Martin's *Untitled #1* (2003), in which there are two black triangles, touching at the base, each ending in a pointed yellow tip.

4 Adelaide Cioni, *To Be Naked. On a Tray*, 2021.

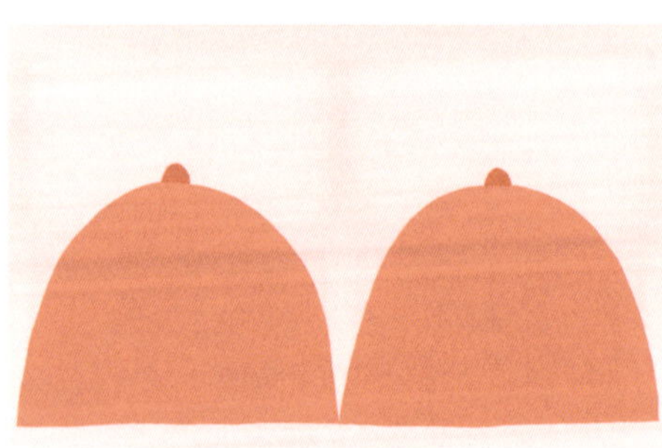

Adelaide Cioni, *To Be Naked. Breasts*, 2020, wool stitched on canvas, 98 × 158 cm

A certain playfulness comes across in *To Be Naked. Legs* (2020), and *To Be Naked. Hand* (2020): the feet are flexed or pointing downwards, the fingers are lightly curved—as if ready to dance or to tickle someone. Not unlike the palms and tropical plants in *Palms*, they are anything but static. The pink flesh which, for Cioni, embodies nakedness, makes for the unity of this body of works. But the artist is well aware that the human body comes in different colours, shapes, and sizes. Published by Les Cerises Editions, *I see me. And you and you and you* (2020), an artist book intended specifically for children, is a case in point. This book project, which grew out of the naked body works, styles itself as "a silent abecedary or a handbook on the body" designed to satisfy children's curiosity about their shape-shifting body and what it will look like once they reach adulthood. Much like Bruno Munari's *Prebooks* and *Illegible Books* from 1949, it contains no words and is meant to be handled, as the fingers on the cover make clear from the outset. One of the spreads inside the book shows an outstretched right arm ending with a hand drawn face down and,

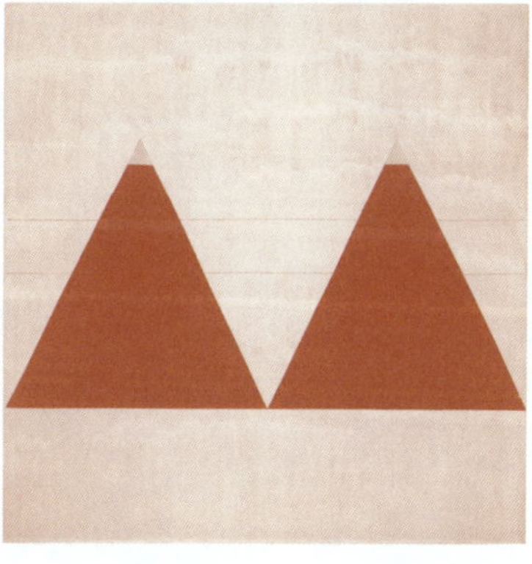

Martin, Agnes, *Untitled #1*, 2003
acrylic and graphite on canvas
152.4 × 152.4 cm, No. 36102

poking out from beneath it, the detailed drawing of the other arm's upturned palm.

It was while swimming naked in the sea that the Futurist poet Filippo Tommaso Marinetti invented Tactilism, or the Art of Touch. Sharing his insights in "reflections of a swimmer," Marinetti describes how he went about educating himself: "I started by submitting my sense of touch to an intensive treatment, pinpointing the confused phenomena of will and thought on various points of my body, and especially on the palms of my hands."[5] Timed to coincide with the centenary of Marinetti's *Manifesto of Tactilism* of 1921, the exhibition *Touching Beauty. Maria Montessori–Bruno Munari* paired two pioneering figures interested in exploring the aesthetic potential of a tactile sensibility, and how to foster it in children.[6] Adelaide Cioni went to a Montessori school, whose educational methods included games that engaged the sense of touch, and her resolutely haptic approach may owe something to these formative experiences. The gallery spaces swathed from floor to ceiling in thin muslin gauzes at Mimosa House, and the hanging fabrics that activate the sense of touch as visitors go through them, hark back to the "tactile rooms" dreamed up by F. T. Marinetti in his mani-

5 F. T. Marinetti, "Il Tattilismo," *Comœdia* (January 1921). An English translation is available here: http://peripheralfocus.net/poems-told-by-touch/manifesto_of_tactilism.html.

6 The exhibition travelled from Museo Tattile Statale Omero in Ancona (8 November 2019–8 March 2020) to Palazzo delle Esposizioni in Rome (22 June 2021–27 February 2022).

festo, inviting the hands of men and women with their diverse sensibilities to set out on a tactile journey together.

References

Cioni, Adelaide, *I see me. And you, and you, and you*. Paris: Les Cerises Editions, 2020.

Lonzi, Carla, *Self-portrait*, transl. Allison Grimaldi Donahue. Brussels and London: Divided Publishing, 2021.

Marinetti, Filippo Tommaso, "Il Tattilismo," *Comœdia* (January 1921).

Munari, Bruno, *Fantasia*. Bari: Editori Laterza, 1977.

Perse, Saint-John, "Pour fêter une enfance," in *Éloges*. Paris: Gallimard, 1948 [1911].

From the Very Beginning

by
Cecilia Canziani

Translated by Sylvia Adrian Notini

During a recent visit to an exhibition about Rome in the Middle Ages, I took a picture of a marble slab with the engraving of a dog with a red and white chequered body, and sent it to Adelaide. A few days later, while she was visiting the same show, Adelaide sent me a photo of a miniature in which a billy goat and a cat stand facing each other playing a harp and a viola, respectively. The fur covering both of their bodies is represented by a repeating identical red pattern. This exchange of images is part of our conversation, and there is no need for an accompanying text: these are encounters in which her work, and mine, come together in a place that we are interested in frequenting because, being marginal, it lets us stop time and even expand it *ad infinitum*, allowing us to touch a motif that, wherever it manifests itself, whatever surface it covers, comes to us from far away, and will probably continue to exist for longer than either of us do. Adelaide Cioni names these "secondary images." They are forms that never constitute the subject of the painting, they remain in the background, but silently, they make their presence heard. And once they have been noticed, they are impossible to forget. Actually, identifying them from painting to painting becomes a way of looking through the images, almost as if to filter their contents in order to compose a history of art as "transmission of marks," stripes and dots after all, represent a sort of ground zero of the composition. I am referring to paintings, but the type of support can be extended to include the fresco, cloth, ceramics. The versatility of the ornamental motifs is also a part of their beauty. From this point of view, time and genres no longer count; all that counts is the irresistible impulse to cover a surface with signs, arranged according to a rhythmical structure that undoubtedly at one time had a precise meaning—sky, sea, world, ship, field—but that remains (and resists) as pure ornament.

You take a sheet of paper and begin making a freehand drawing of a horizontal line. Then another, just below it. And you continue that way, keeping the same distance between the two marks. Once a certain number of horizontal lines has been made, you continue by making vertical lines, to create a checkerboard. At this point you can choose one or more colours and start filling the pattern, alternating them.

On the occasion of one exhibition we worked on together, we hung this drawing on the side of a column, at the centre of the exhibition space. A discreet presence that conversed with a tapestry on the same subject and the other large-scale works made of cloth that featured—together with *Go Easy on Me*—the first polysemic shapes: *Il mare* (2019) or a sequence of wavy blue lines, *Il sole* (2019) or a yellow disk, *I buchi neri* (2019) or four ellipses that grow smaller in size, and a cylindrical yellow sculpture or *Colonna* (2019).

In a certain sense, the small drawing of the checkerboard seemed to remain suspended between the state of the finished work and the scale model. These days, as I look at the images of the exhibition, I realise that the drawing is not just in conversation with every single work on display, but it is actually its barycentre. An image that organises the space around itself.

The reflections on "secondary images" then took a more specific direction when transported to another type of support. They become a sampling of signs etched on photographic film and then projected as diaposlides. This means they can be of different dimensions, and coincide with the wall on

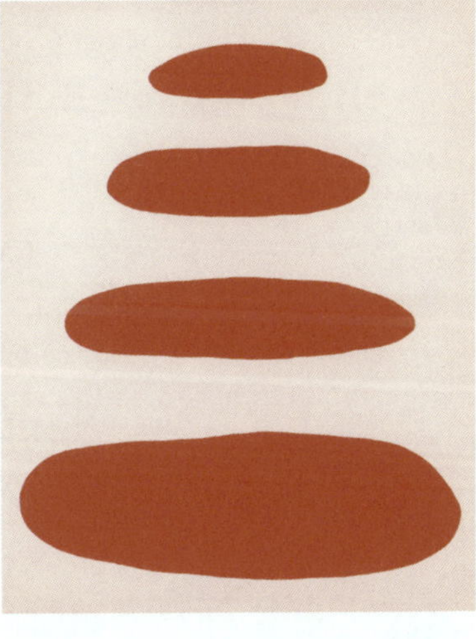

Adelaide Cioni, *I buchi neri*, 2019, wool stitched on canvas, 150 × 120 cm

which they are projected, while remaining almost immaterial. As close as possible to an original form to conform to. Because when all is said and done this is what it is: an "exercise in translation." Which is the title, among other things, of a series of acrylics on paper whose subject is the portrait (I use this term deliberately) or the declination in another medium of a chequered cloth in which the pattern of the warp and the woof also, inevitably and ironically, evokes the Modernist grid.

Translating always means placing in between the original text and its restitution one's own subjectivity; this is why every version of a pattern—a given and consolidated form that does not involve invention—is always the same. The almost imperceptible difference is the visible trace of the person who appropriated for themselves an ornamental motif, and then reproduced it. I believe that this is the reason why one can be moved before a piece of cloth painted four thousand years ago by an anonymous painter.[1] And choose to turn these "secondary images," *parerga*, into the subject of the painting: to record one's uniqueness, in as direct a manner as possible. This explains why Adelaide always makes a freehand drawing of the work,

1 As Adelaide says, "Painting is a way of being in the world, of relating to a certain materiality of things. Painters like to get dirty, normally, they like being immersed in that sticky material that is paint. It is a visceral thing. I recently saw at the Museo Egizio in Turin what is considered the oldest painting on cloth to have survived. It is touching to look at, touching to think that we are still here four thousand years later trying to put something meaningful on a piece of cloth." https://www.artribune.com/professioni-e-professionisti/who-is-who/2020/11/pittura-intervista-adelaide-cioni/.

so that she can give back, or rather record, what she calls her personal vibration, a term that I am fond of because it introduces the idea of the rhythm and sound that brings to life her most recent works consisting solely of stripes, dots, and waves.

I believe, in any case, that the reason why Adelaide creates stripes, dots, and waves is because they make her feel joy. This brings to mind something that Winifred Nicholson once said:

> "I like painting flowers—I have tried to paint many things in many different ways, but my paint brush always gives a tremor of pleasure when I let it paint a flower—and I think I know why this is so. Flowers mean different things to different people—to some they are trophies to decorate their dwellings (for this plastic flowers will do as well as real ones)—to some they are buttonholes for their conceit—to botanists they are species and tabulated categories—to bees of course they are honey—to me they are the secret of the cosmos."[2]

Painting flowers—many flowers—painting dots or stripes—many dots or stripes—, bestows a special happiness, because it connects the gesture of the

2 Crane Kalman Gallery, *The Flowers of Winifred Nicholson* (London: Crane Kalman Gallery, 1969) and reprinted as "The Flower's Response" in Winifred Nicholson, *Unknown Colour: Paintings, Letters, Writings*, ed. Andrew Nicholson (London: Faber and Faber, 1987).

artist who makes it (and who chooses their sign, and repeats it, chasing it *ad infinitum*) to the structure of the universe. For Adelaide, drawing geometric motifs is a way of relating to nature, borrowing its method—each tree is made up of leaves, and each leaf is different, just as each of the lines left by the artist on the canvas is different—but it also means representing what, in our finiteness, we do not know how to measure (after all, the word "ornament" comes from "order").

I interrupted my writing to read a few pages written by Agnes Martin. What for Nicholson is a tremor, and for Adelaide a vibration, for Martin is inspiration, the ability to grasp an image the moment it comes to one's mind and to fix it on the canvas.

> "When I draw horizontals
> you see this big plane and you have
> certain feelings like
> you're expanding over the plane
> Anything can be painted without
> representation.[3]"

For Adelaide, in a similar way to Martin and Nicholson, drawing does not mean inventing a form, neither in a strict sense by making a copy of it,

3 Agnes Martin, *Writings* (Berlin: Hatje Cantz, 2005), 37.

and even less so by making a representation of it, where the structure would become symbol and thus story. Rather, it is the attempt to recreate on the canvas the profound connection that exists between the human being and the universe. Martin uses a simple, final word to define this passage: *beauty*. Part of that beauty is the artist's body, through which signs take shape in the world, and themselves become bodies—all different, all unique.

Recently, the patterns Adelaide draws have begun to lose their materiality and acquire spatiality. It may seem like a contradiction, but what I want to say is that the signs—which resist being a representation by way of repetition and reduction and by becoming increasingly less complex, original structures, impressed on gauze or some lightweight cloth—become mobile and capable of adhering to a given milieu (becoming space) or of bestowing a space with a temporary shape.

In this sense *Six or Seven* (2019) is a work that marks an important development. This work, produced in a small church in Spoleto, is inspired by its upper register, frescoed with a Virgin Enthroned and Saints. The iconography of Our Lady of Mercy and of Our Lady of the Nativity point to a coincidence, in Italian Renaissance tradition, between the body of the Virgin and the body of the Church. In the fifteenth century, the female body—which is space to the nth degree—draped in robes, was as unknowable and mysterious as the language of gestures was explicit.

Inside this space, Adelaide built a practicable architectural structure consisting of vertical modules and a canvas canopy, painted in thick red stripes. From outside, the structure, which is visible from the windows that open out onto the facade, resembles a curtain of the kind that we find in Giotto's frescoes: it is an idea of architecture. Upon entering the church, we are contained inside this *camera picta*, which actually prevents you from seeing the original space. Clearly visible on the canvases are the hands that translate and isolate the gestures of the Virgin and the Saints. Hence, in this work a system of signs overlaps another, resisting any narrative drift, because neither of the two codes is capable of speaking to us, today. Abstract gestures and signs thus harken back to a common memory that, precisely in that territory filled with the works of Giotto, Piero della Francesca, and Perugino, is so alive. They tell us nothing, but they are language.

The chance to leave the plane opened up by this work, resides in a performative, modular, impermanent screen in *Modules* (2021), and in *Cape and Modules* (2021): a painting to be worn, where the corpus of signs is once again a body.

Until, in a series of live performances involving drawing and music where the artist's hand translates the sound into sign, there is a further passage. The drawing is freed from the support via the use of gauze—lightweight, transparent, almost devoid of weight and material—and it becomes space, and the pattern, already intuited as being a rhythmical structure starting from the first works on secondary forms, wholly becomes movement. An embodied sign that visualises in space the vibration that is the song of the world.

References:
Gullì, Damiano, *Pittura lingua morta. Intervista ad Adelaide Cioni*. https://www.artribune.com/professioni-e-professionisti/who-is-who/2020/11/pittura-intervista-adelaide-cioni/ (accessed 13 February 2022).
Martin, Agnes, *Writings*. Berlin: Hatje Cantz Verlag, 2005.
Nicholson, Winifred, *Unknown Colour: Paintings, Letters, Writings*, ed. Andrew Nicholson. London: Faber and Faber, 1987.

In my painting, I try to “create bodies” and appeal to the viewer’s body by using fabric, especially wool, possibly thick, sometimes hairy, because I rely on my experience and I know that as soon as I see them I get the urge to touch them. And it’s the same thing I see happening to people who approach my works. They ask me “May I?”

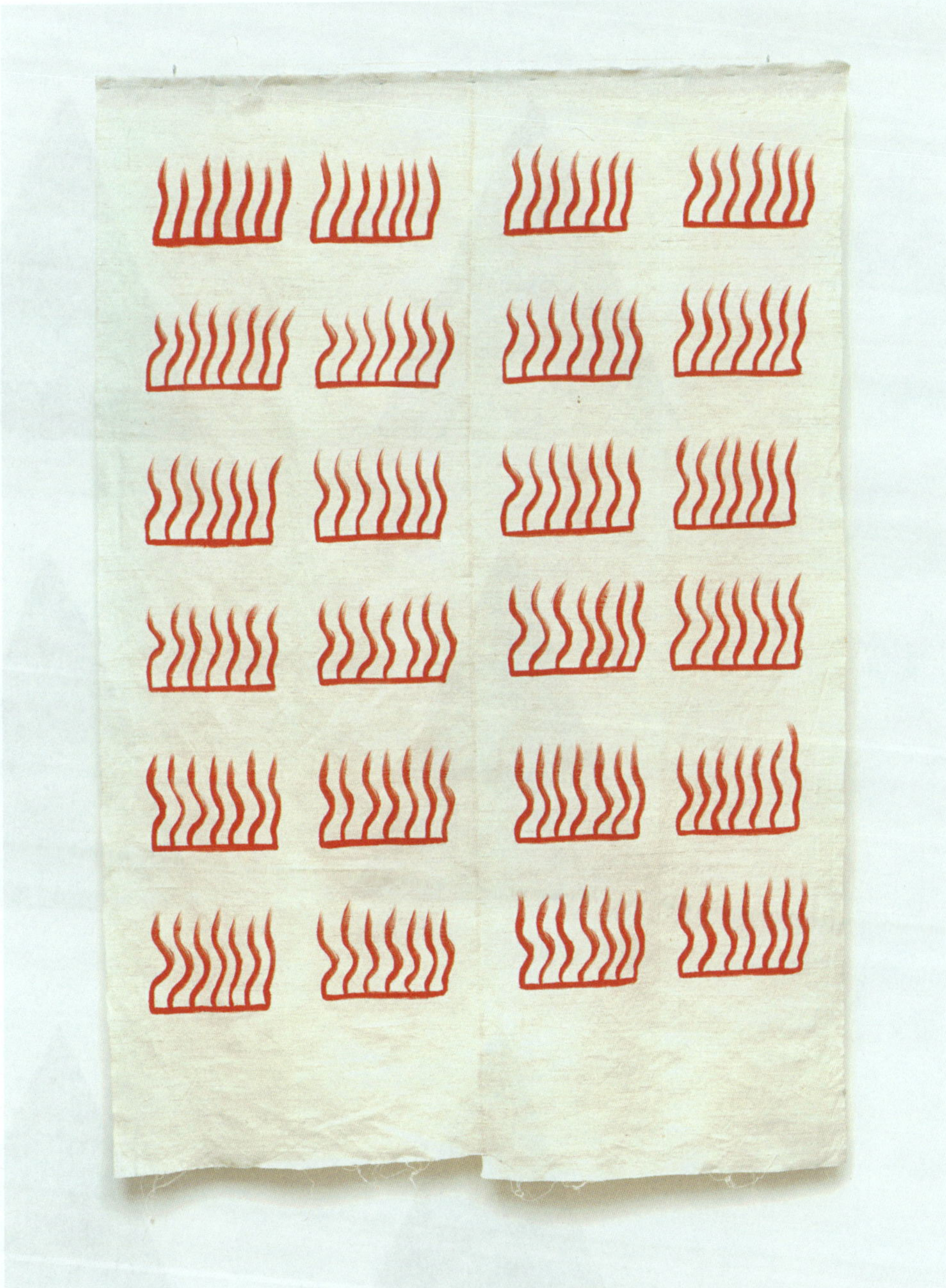

Song for the Fire, 2023, vinyl paint on linen, 164 × 114 cm

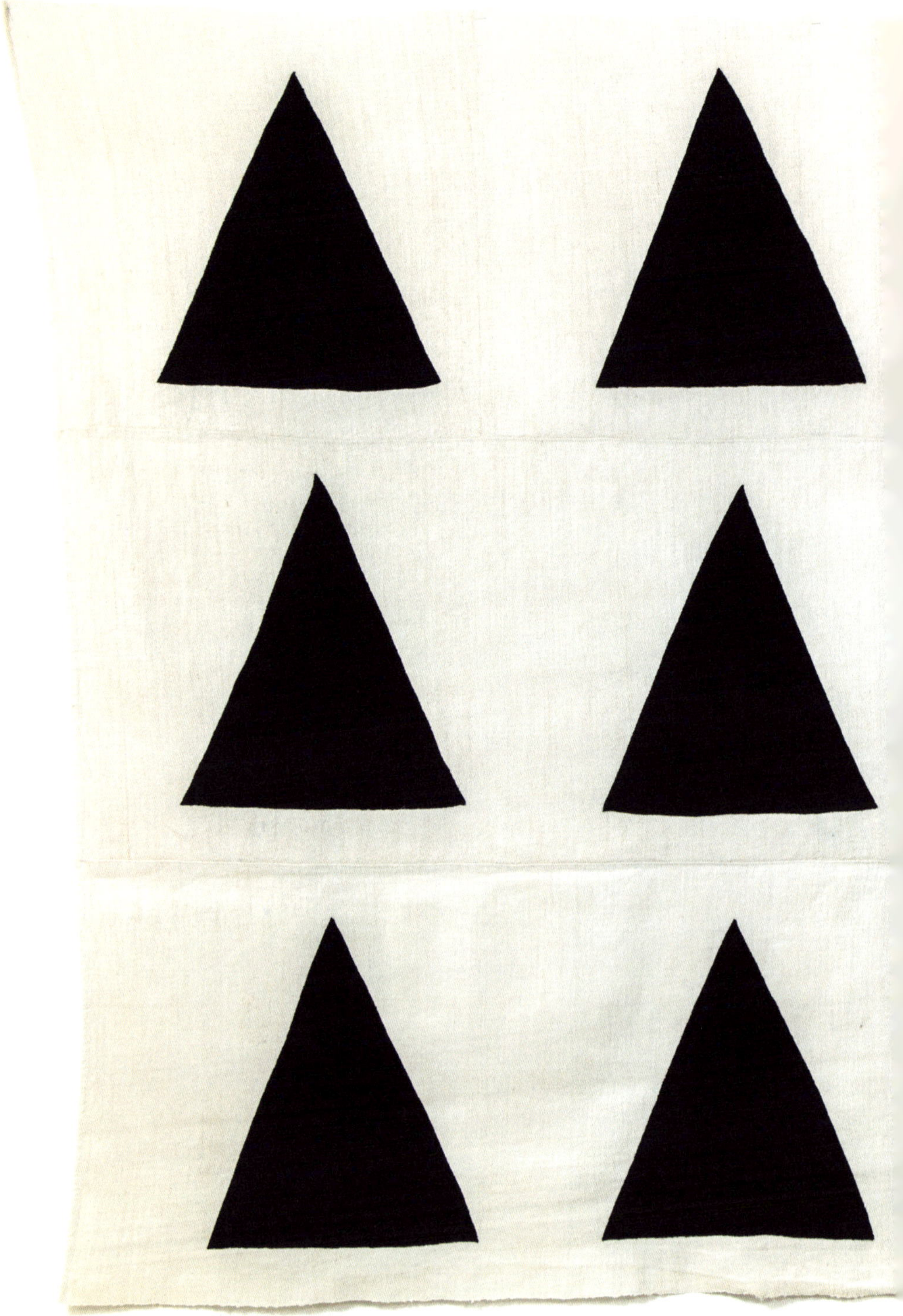

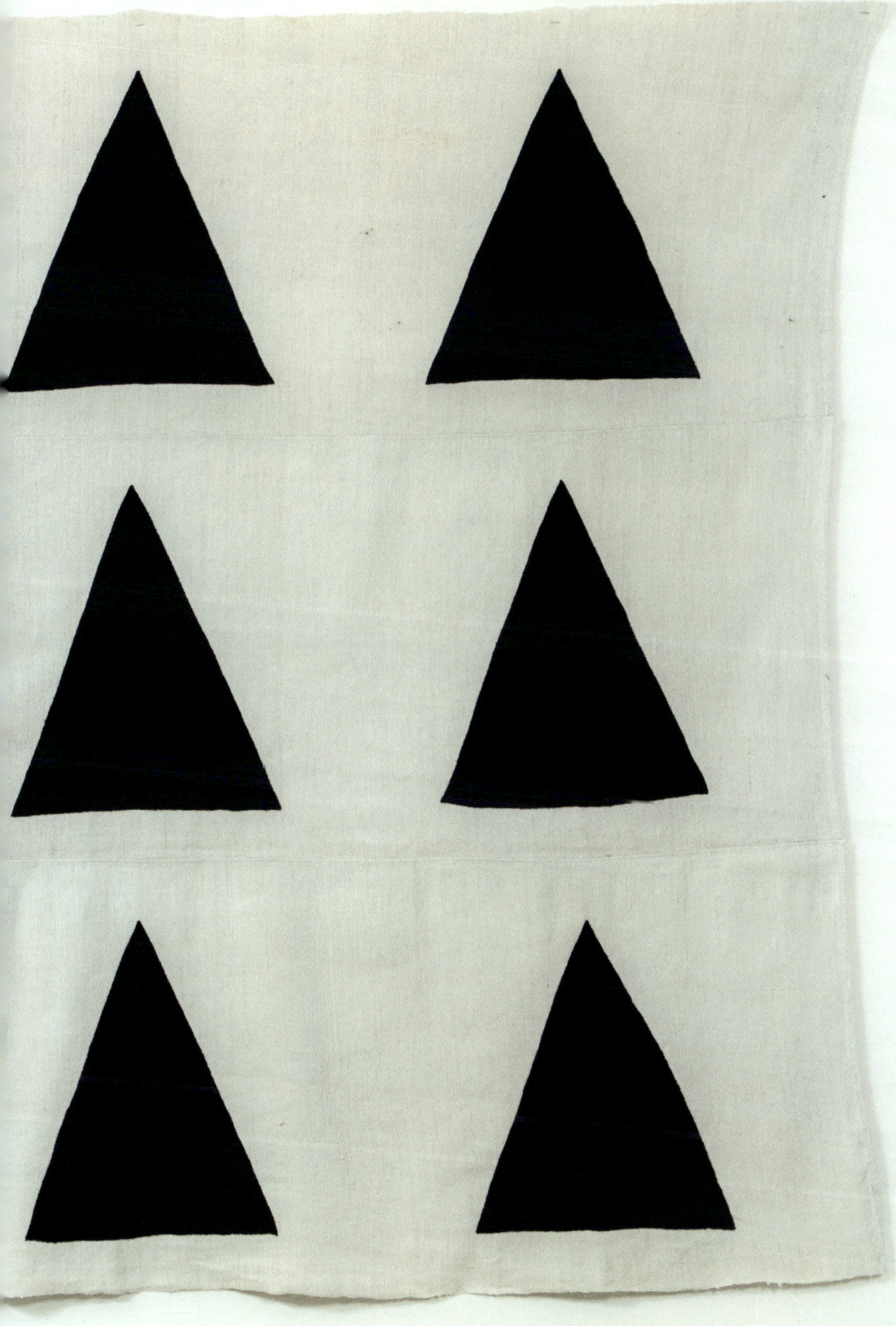

Ab Ovo. Black Triangles, 2023, wool stitched on linen, 144 × 201 cm

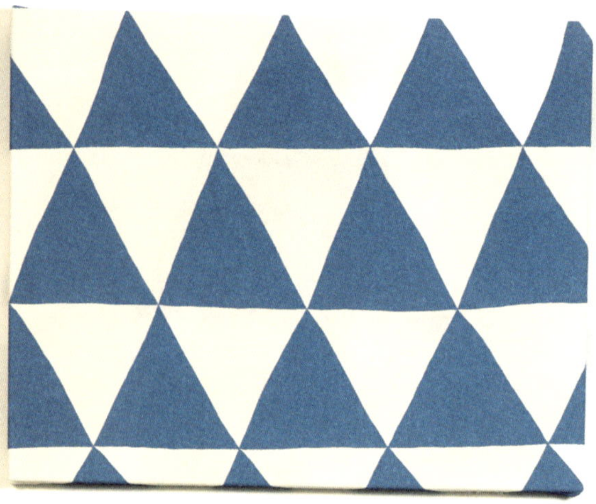

Drawings for Myself. Blue Triangles, 2023,
 vinyl paint and pencil on canvas, 55 × 65cm

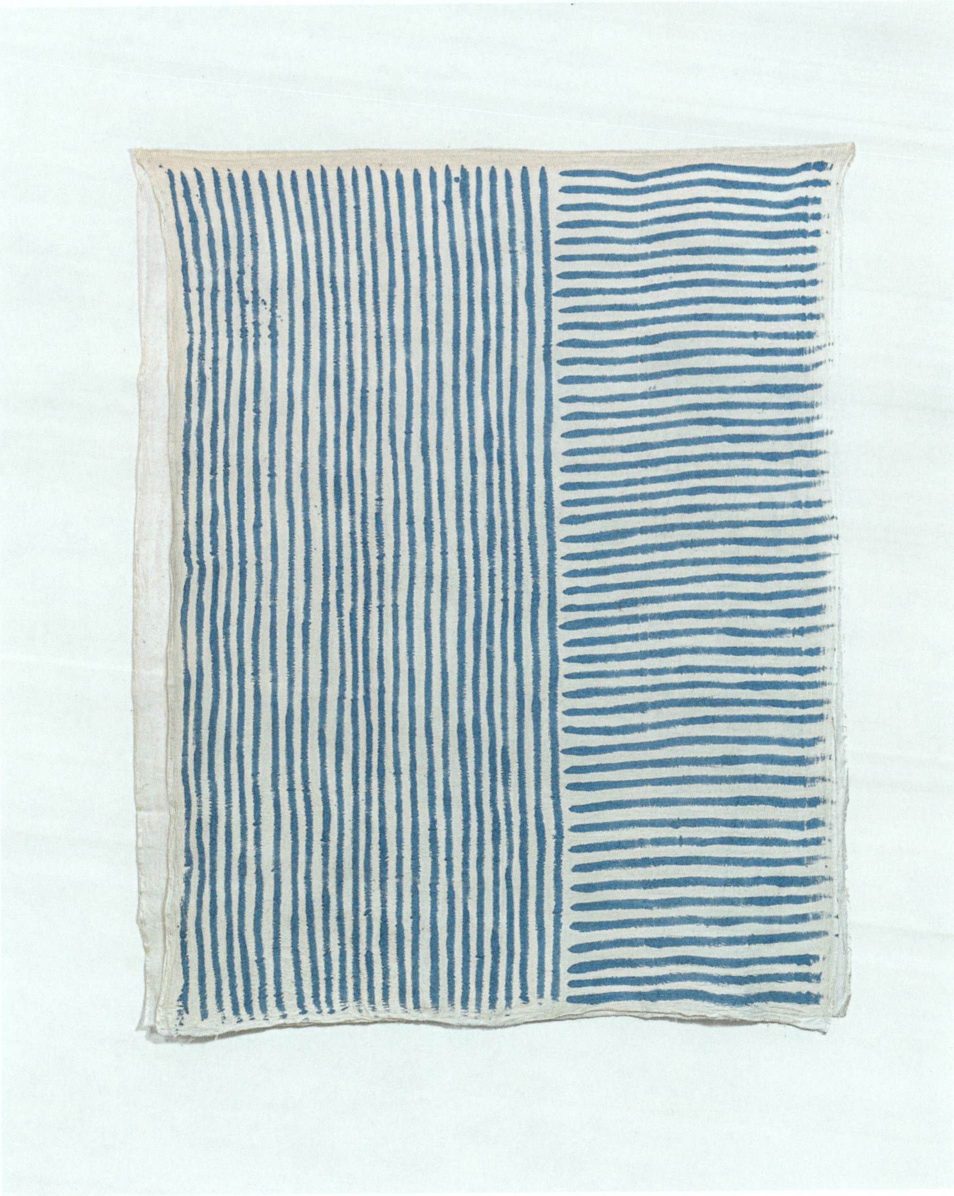

Song of the Blue Lines, 2021, vinyl paint on muslin, 173 × 145 cm

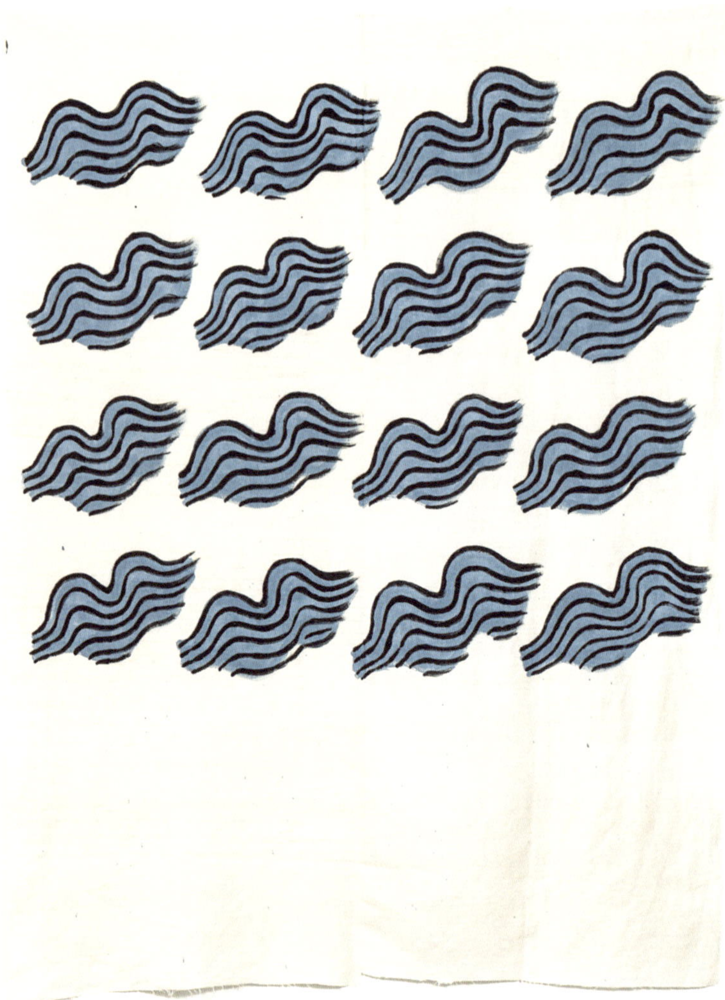

Song for the Sea, 2023, vinyl paint on linen,
182 × 138 cm

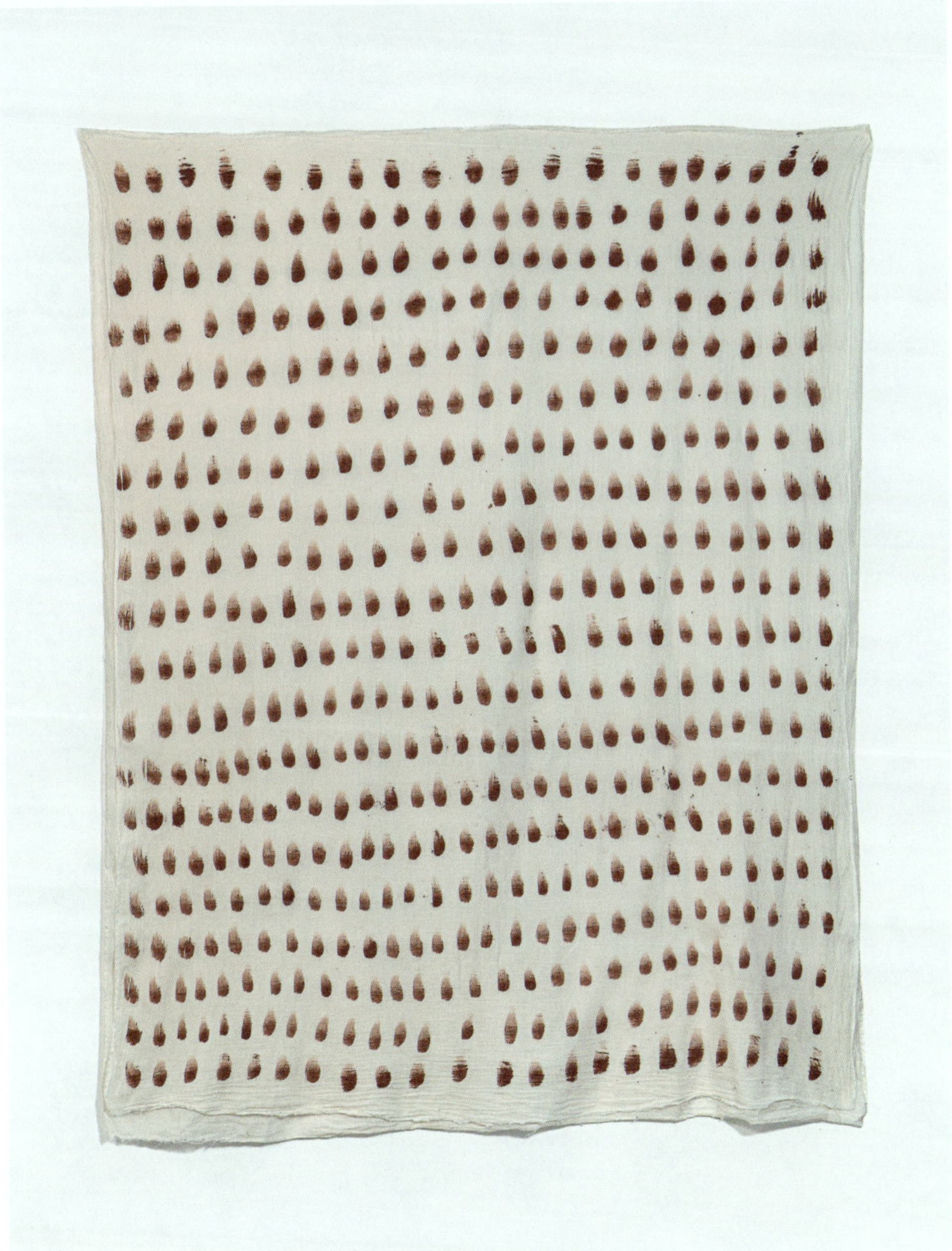

Song of the Red Dots, 2021, vinyl paint on muslin, 178 × 143 cm

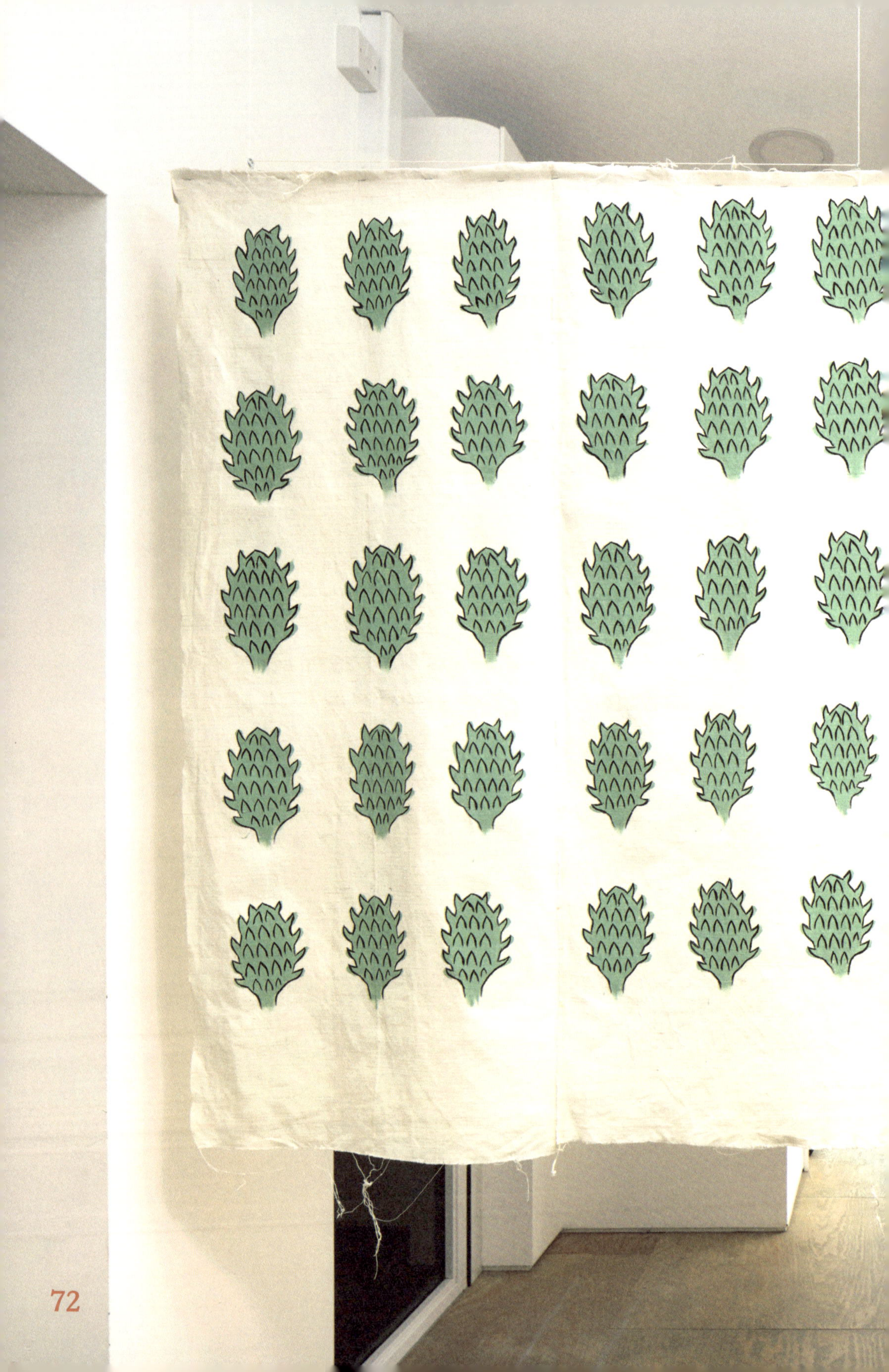

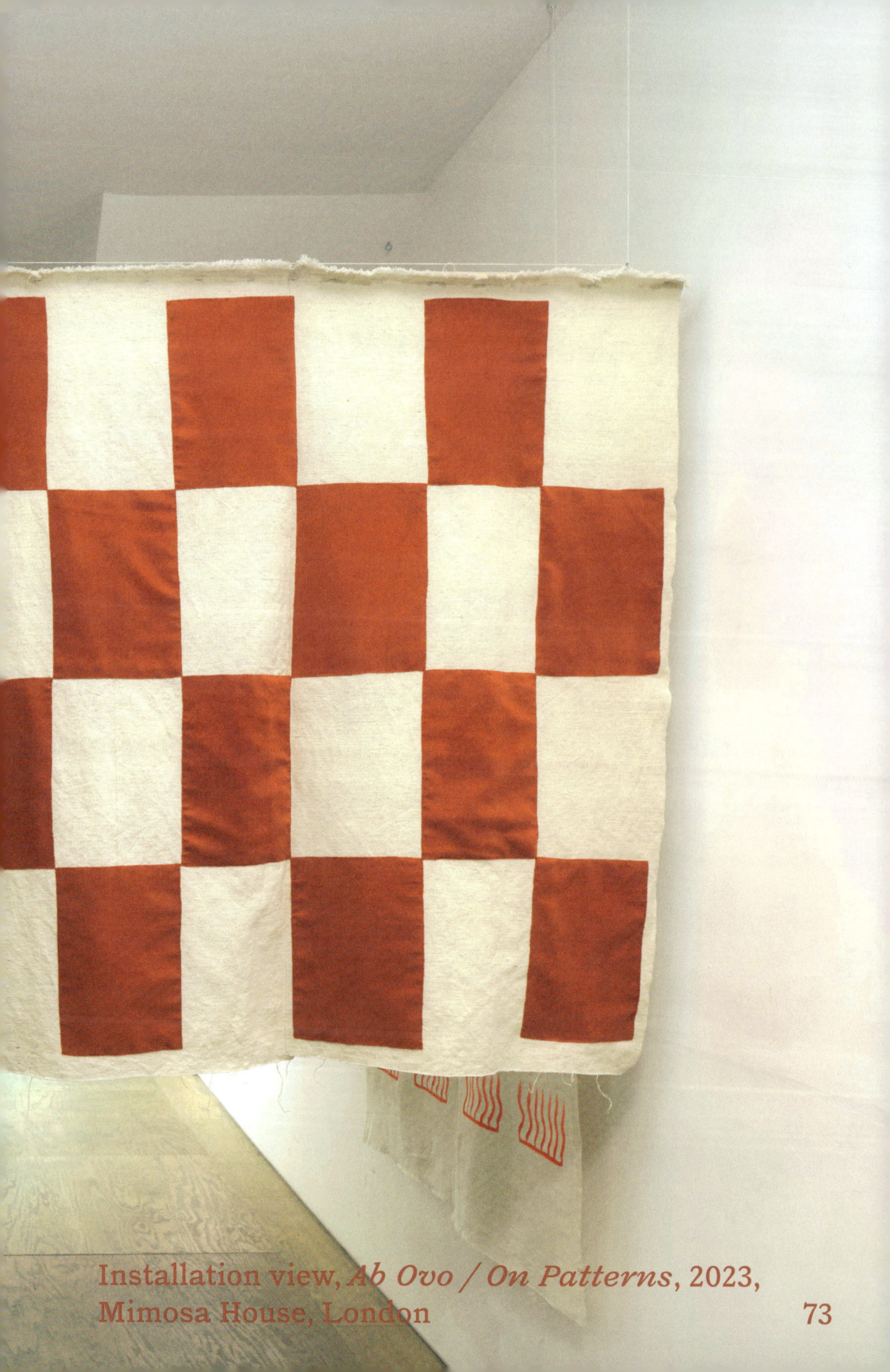

Installation view, *Ab Ovo / On Patterns*, 2023, Mimosa House, London

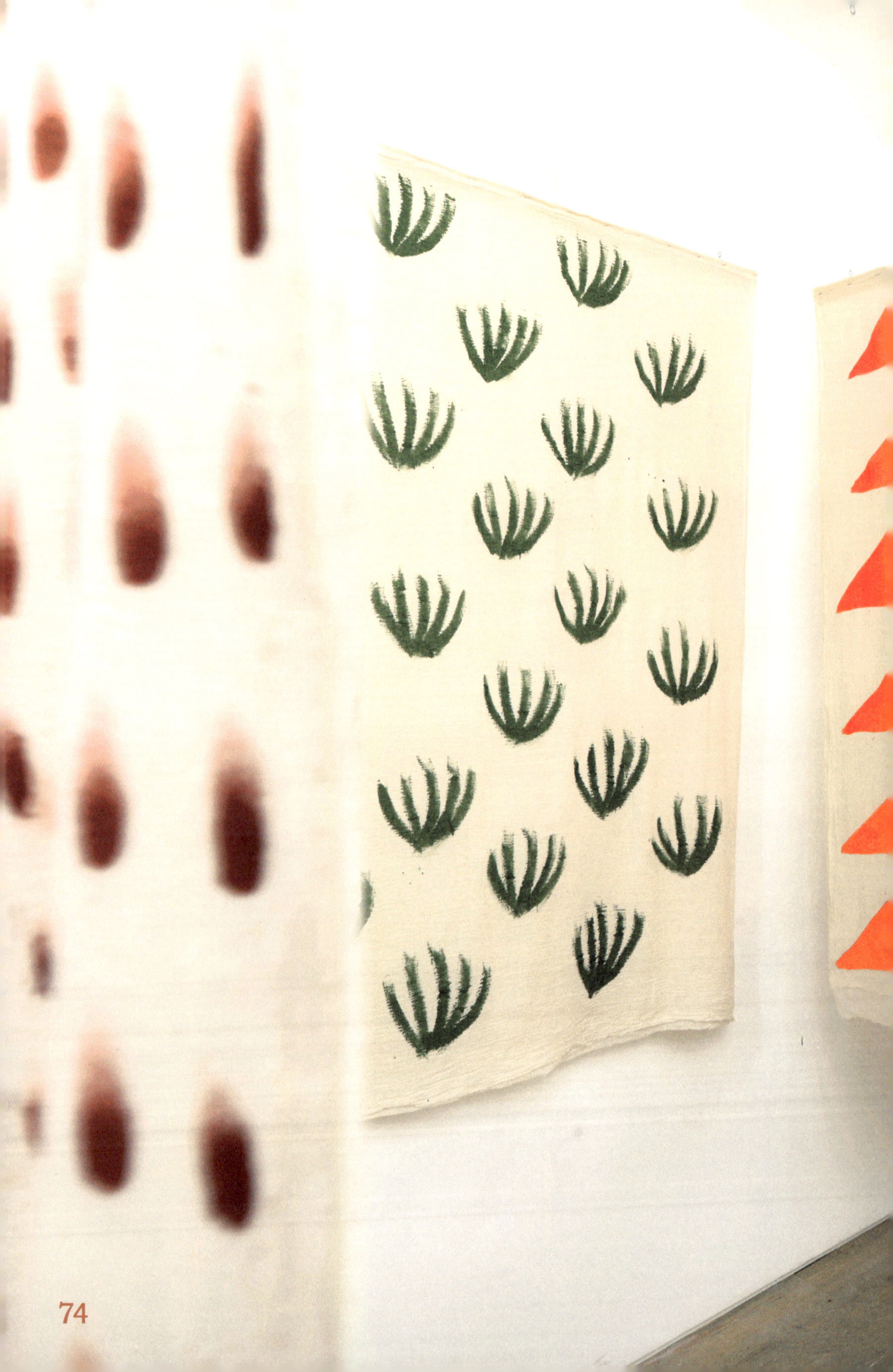

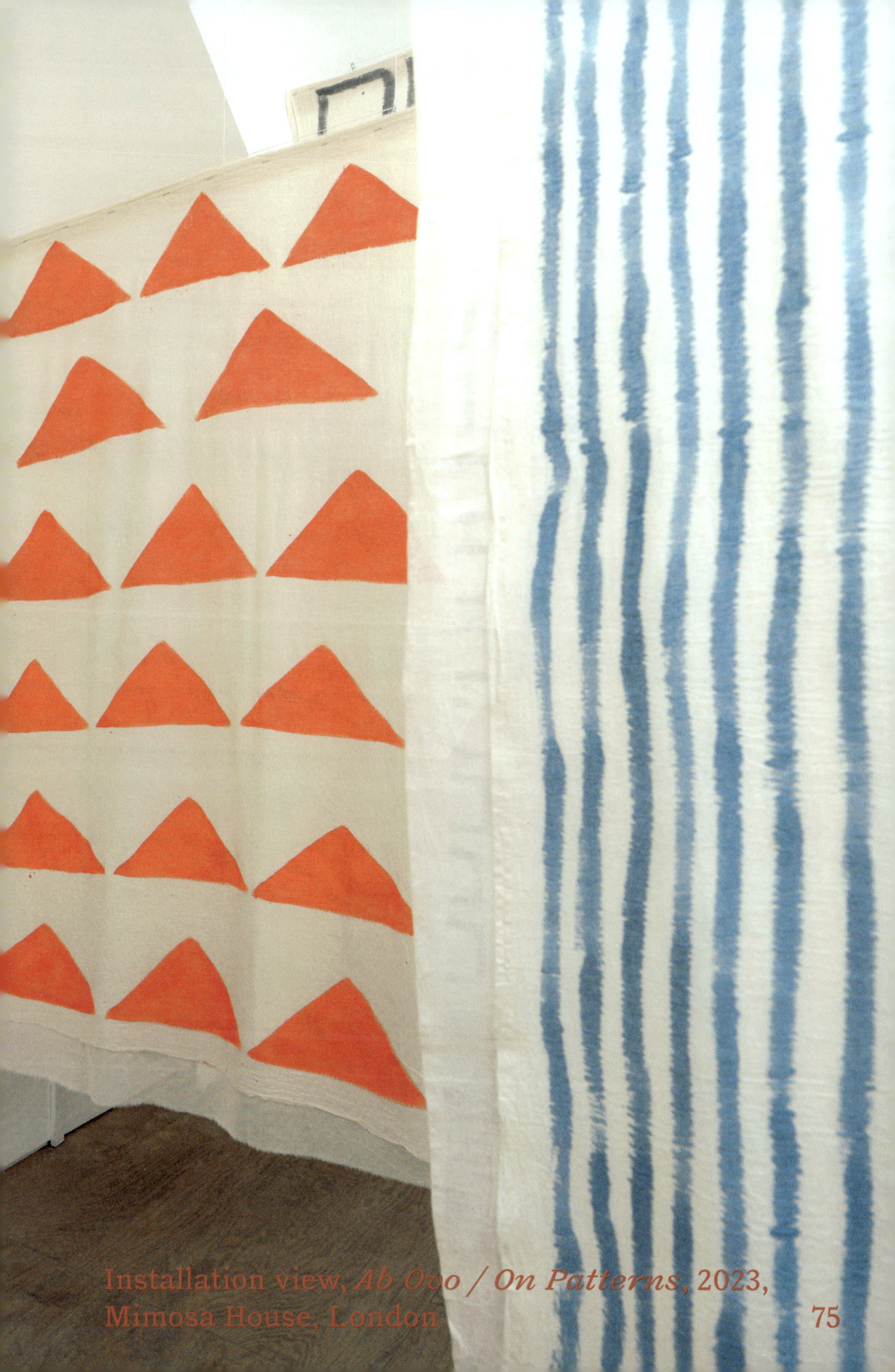

Installation view, *Ab Ovo / On Patterns*, 2023, Mimosa House, London

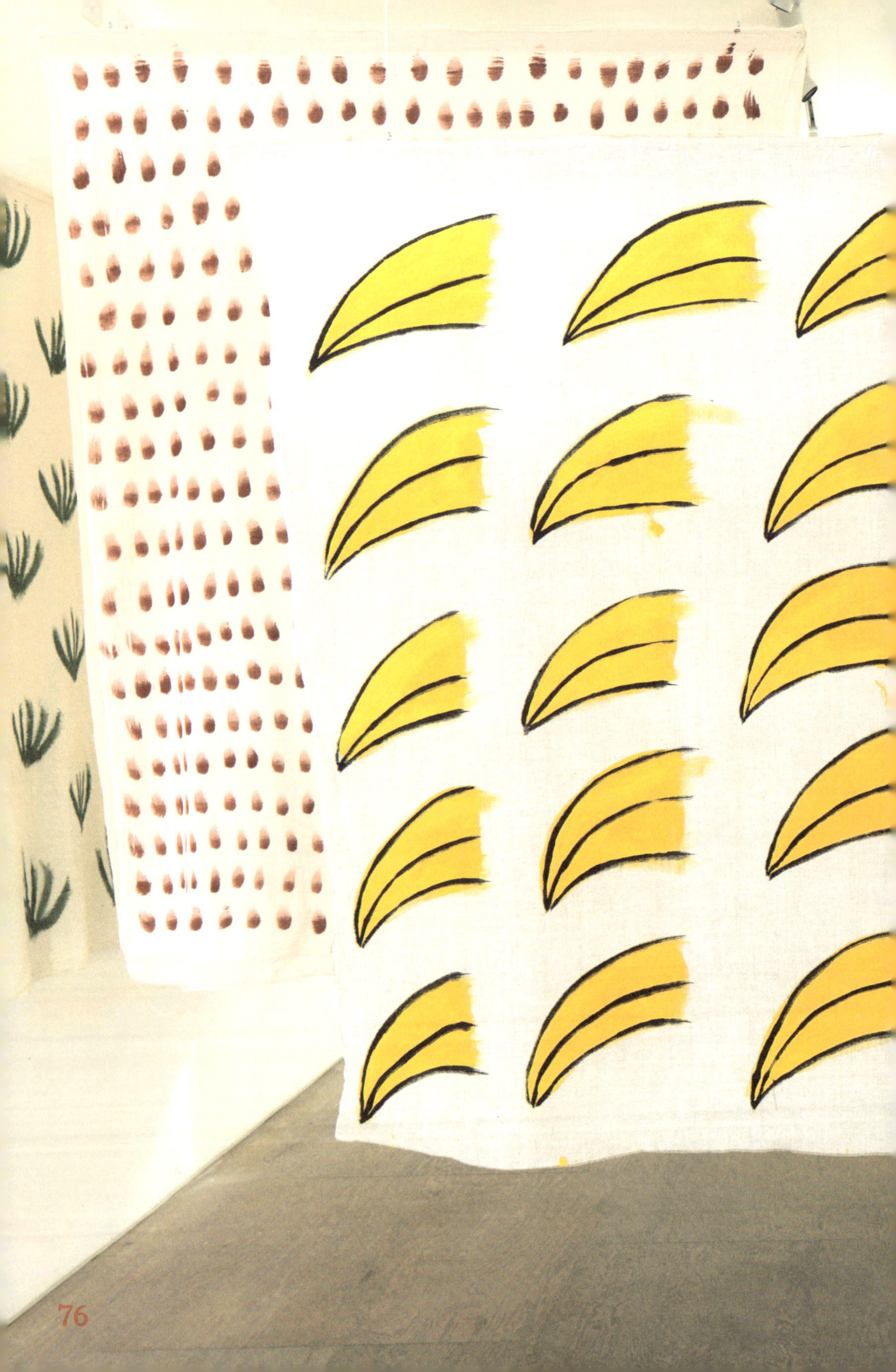

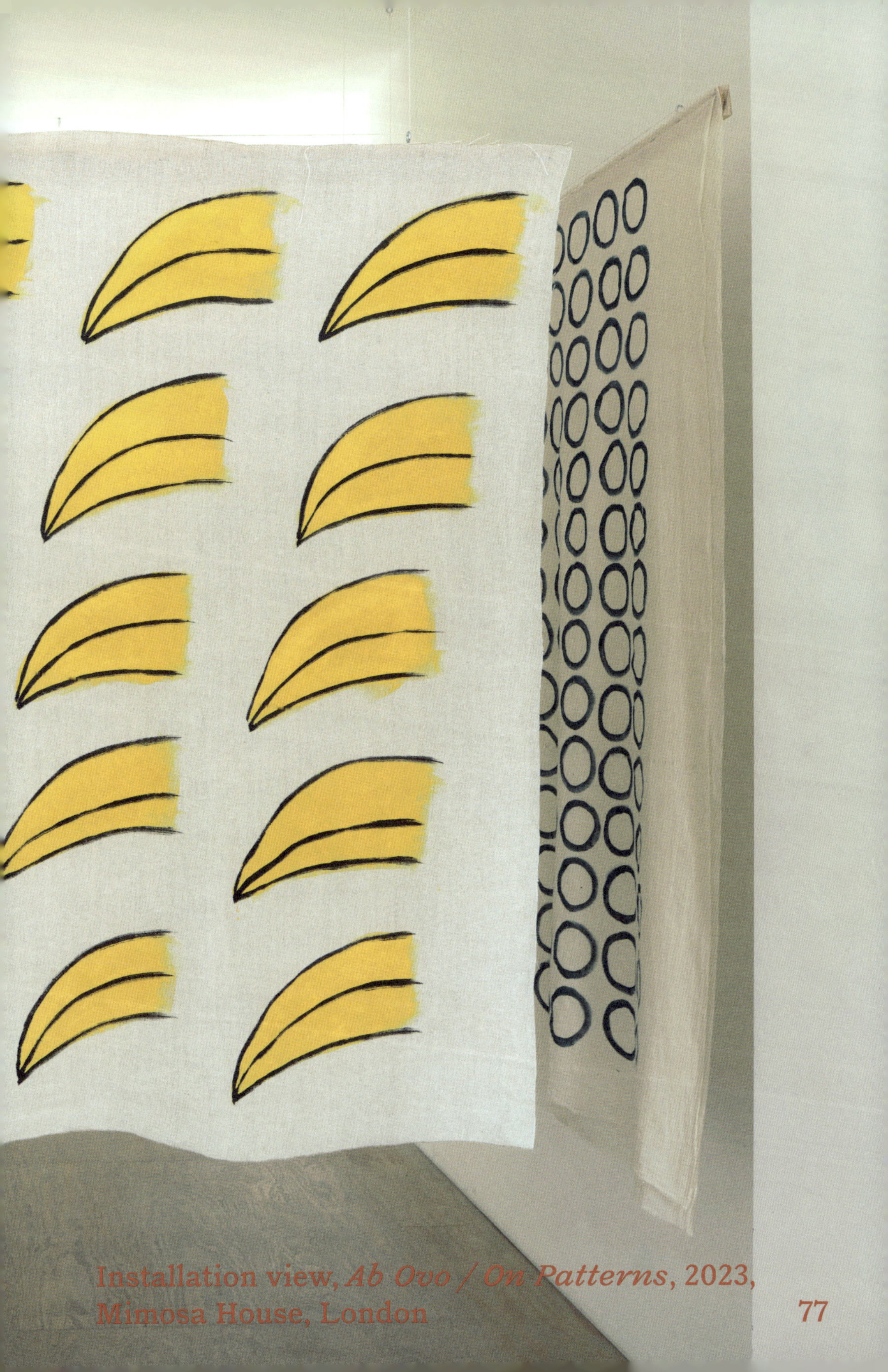

Installation view, *Ab Ovo / On Patterns*, 2023, Mimosa House, London

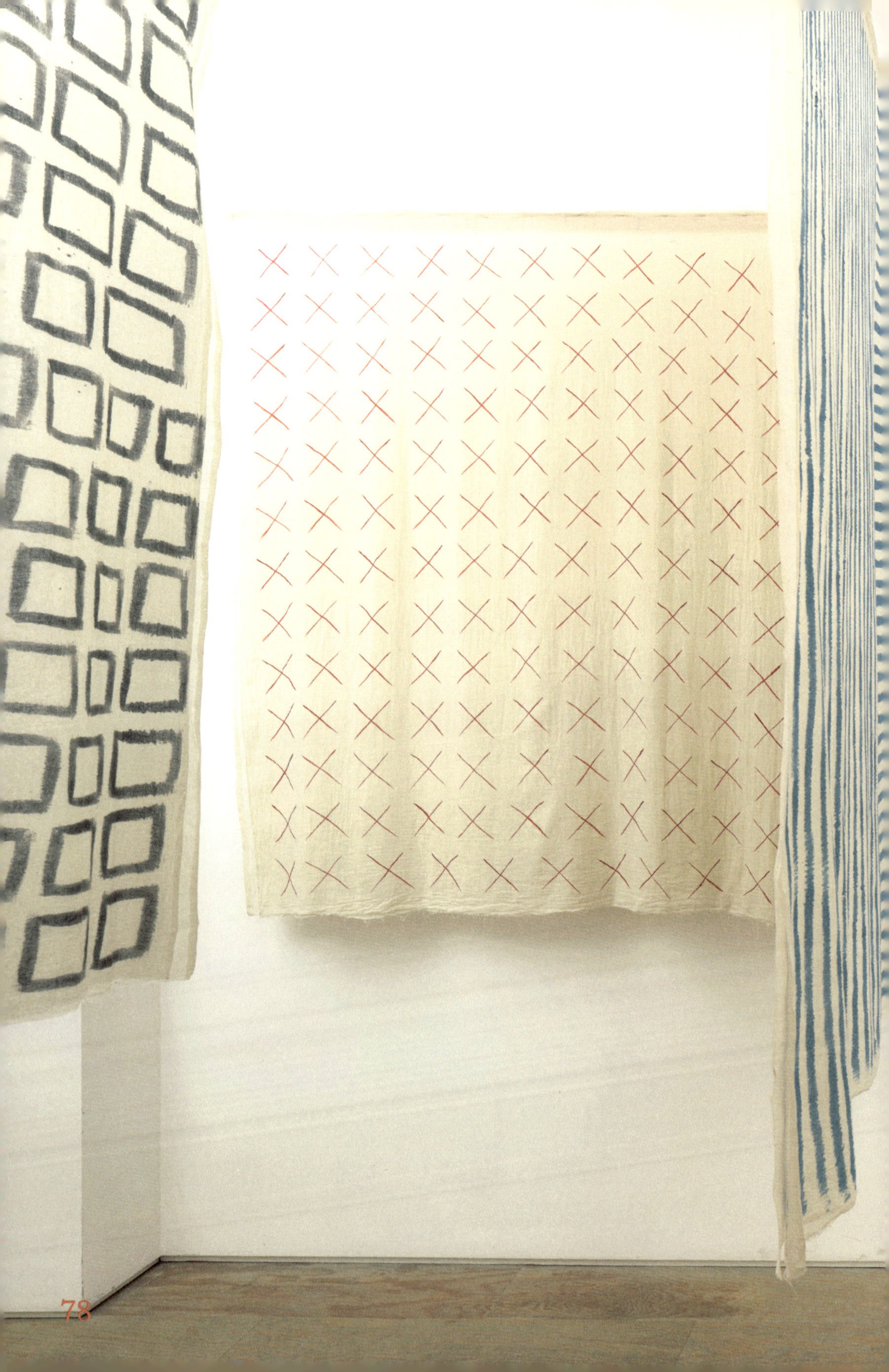

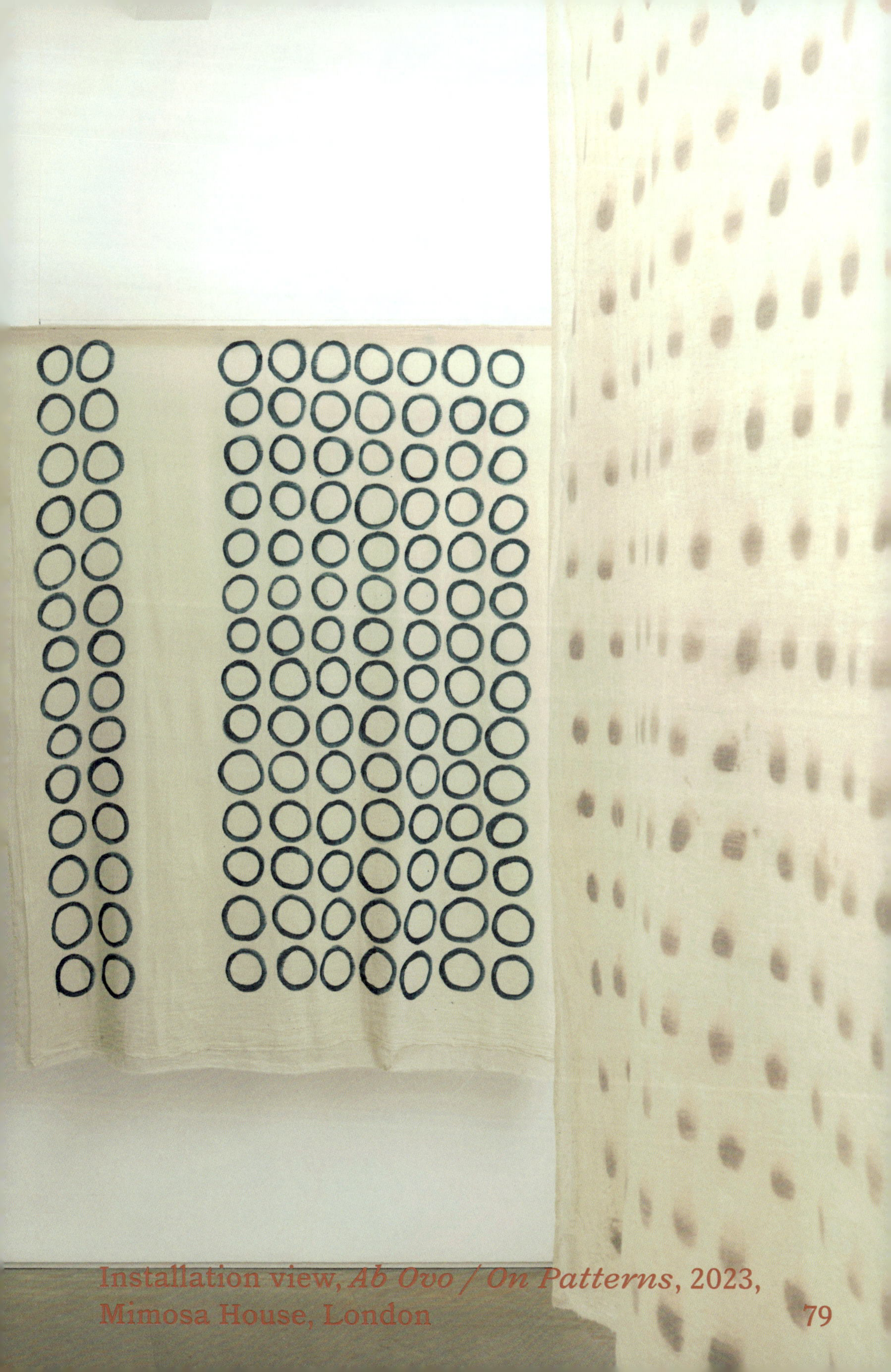

Installation view, *Ab Ovo / On Patterns*, 2023, Mimosa House, London

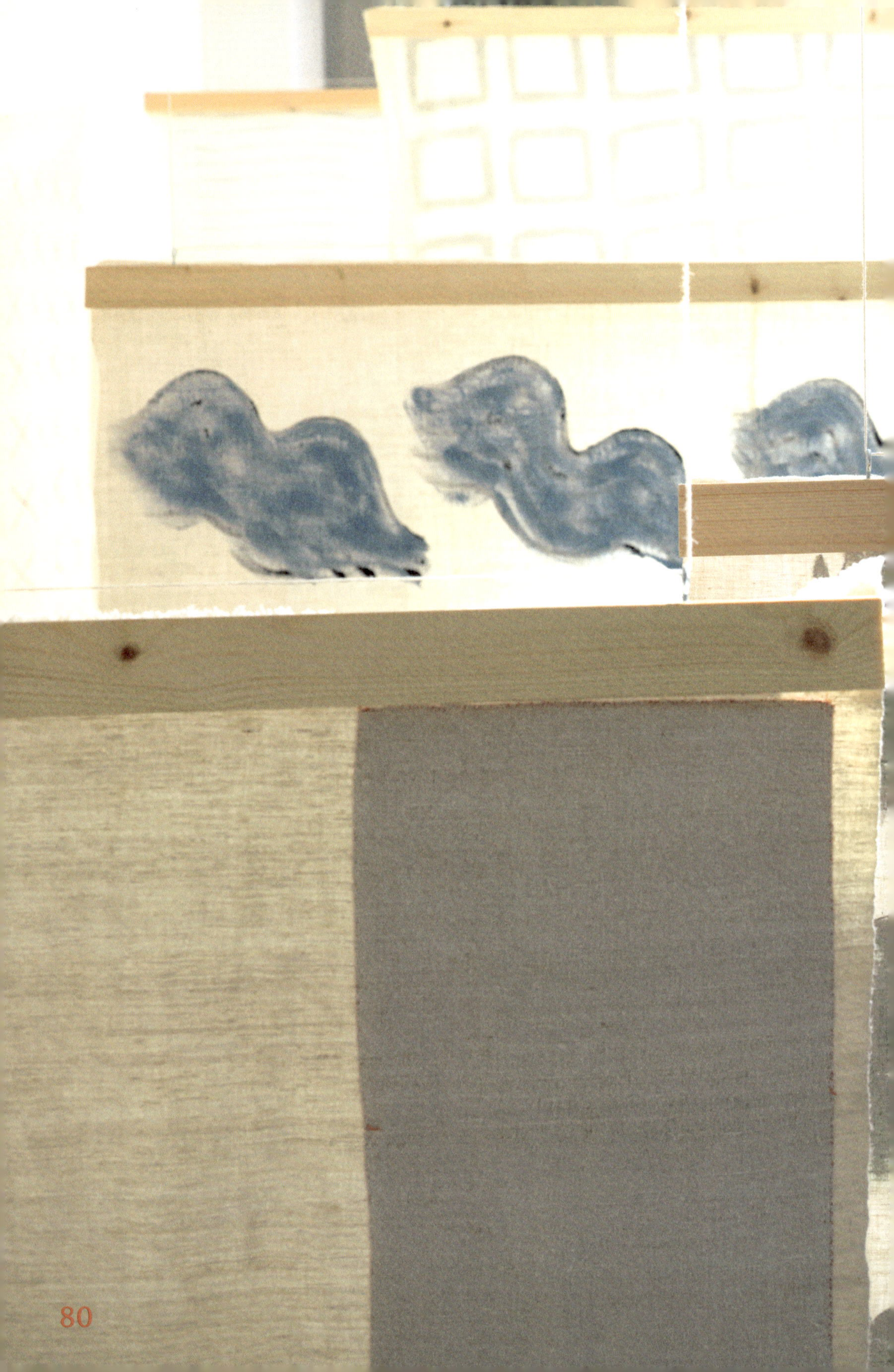

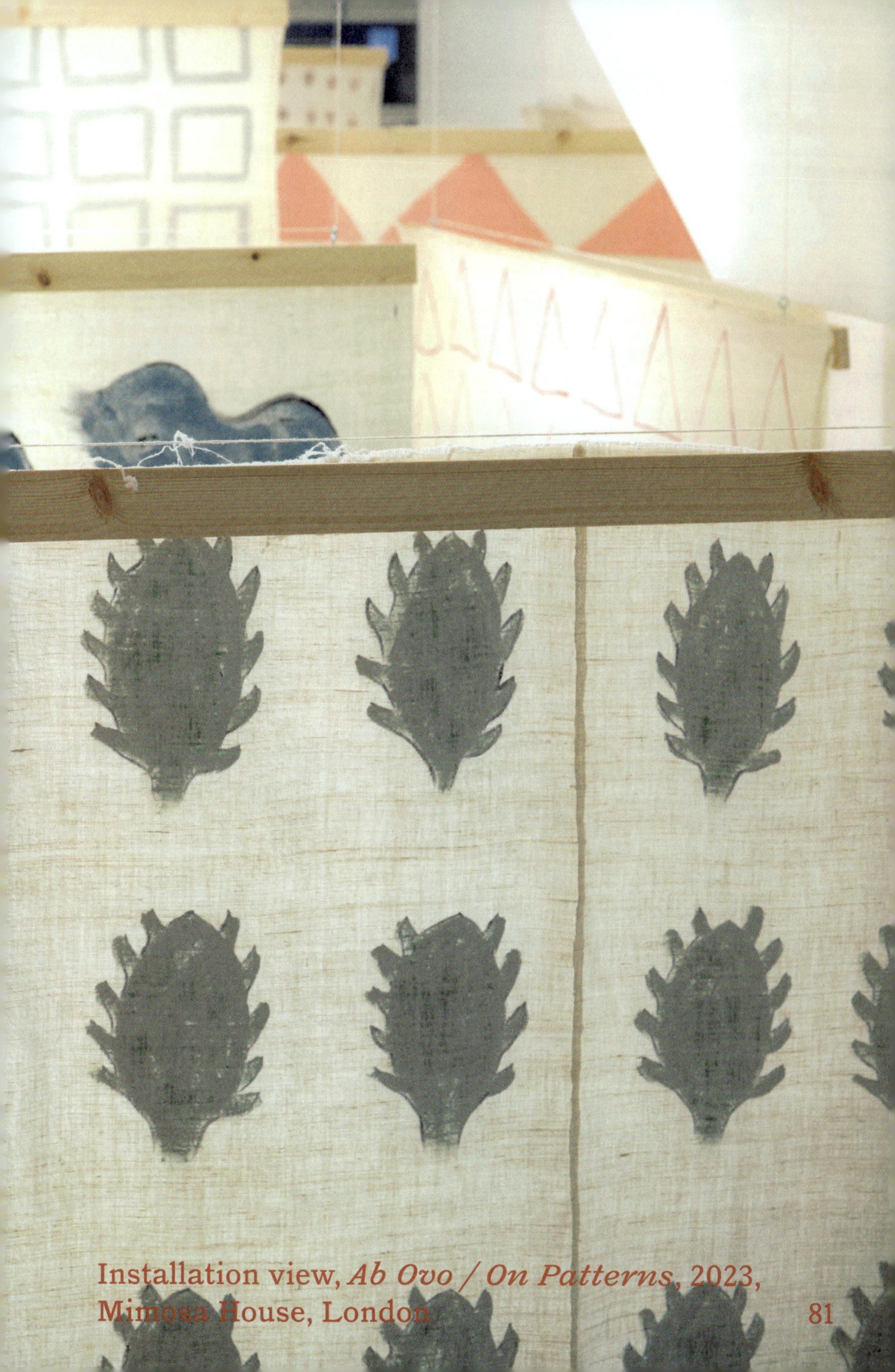

Installation view, *Ab Ovo / On Patterns*, 2023,
Mimosa House, London

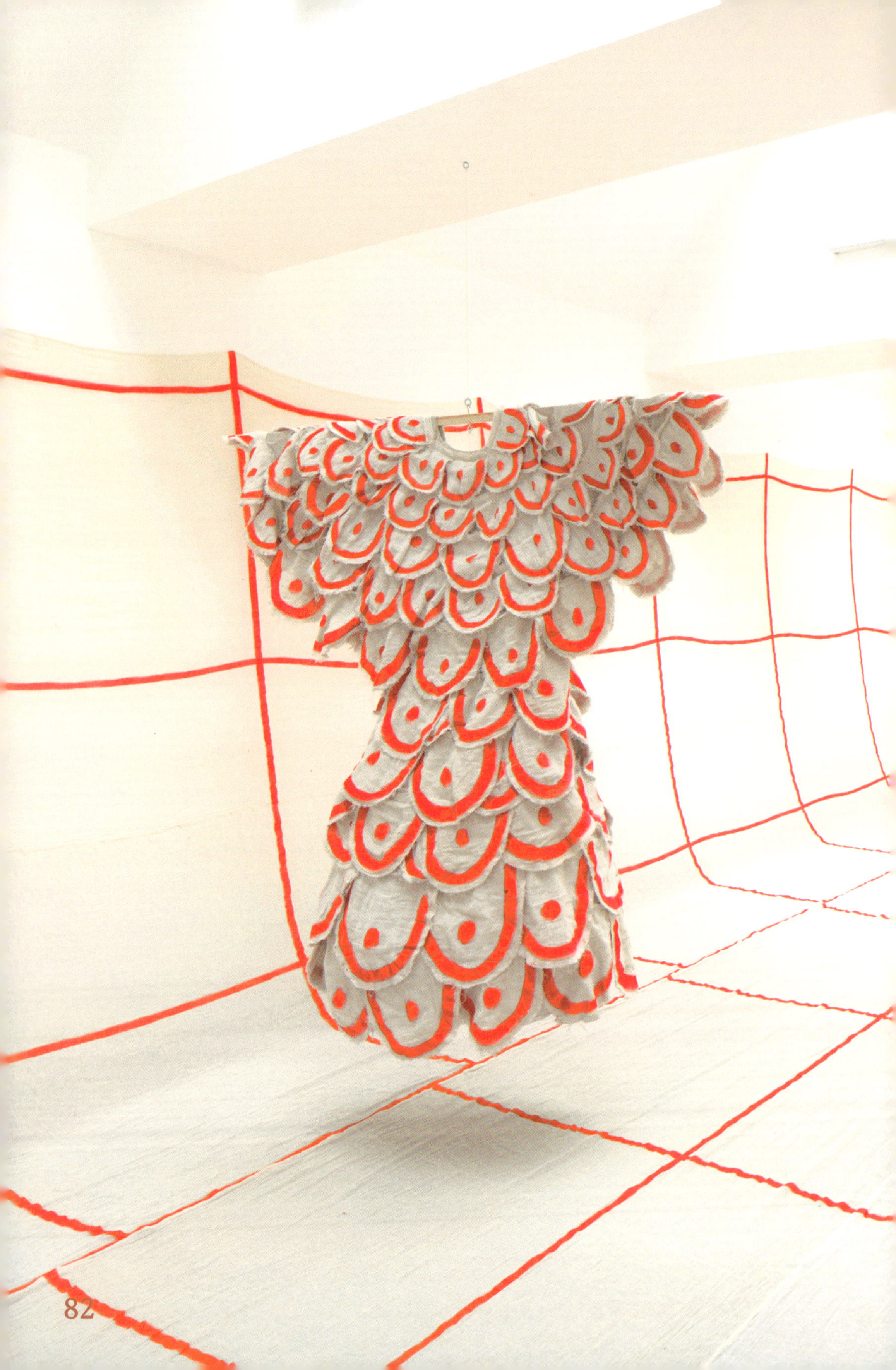

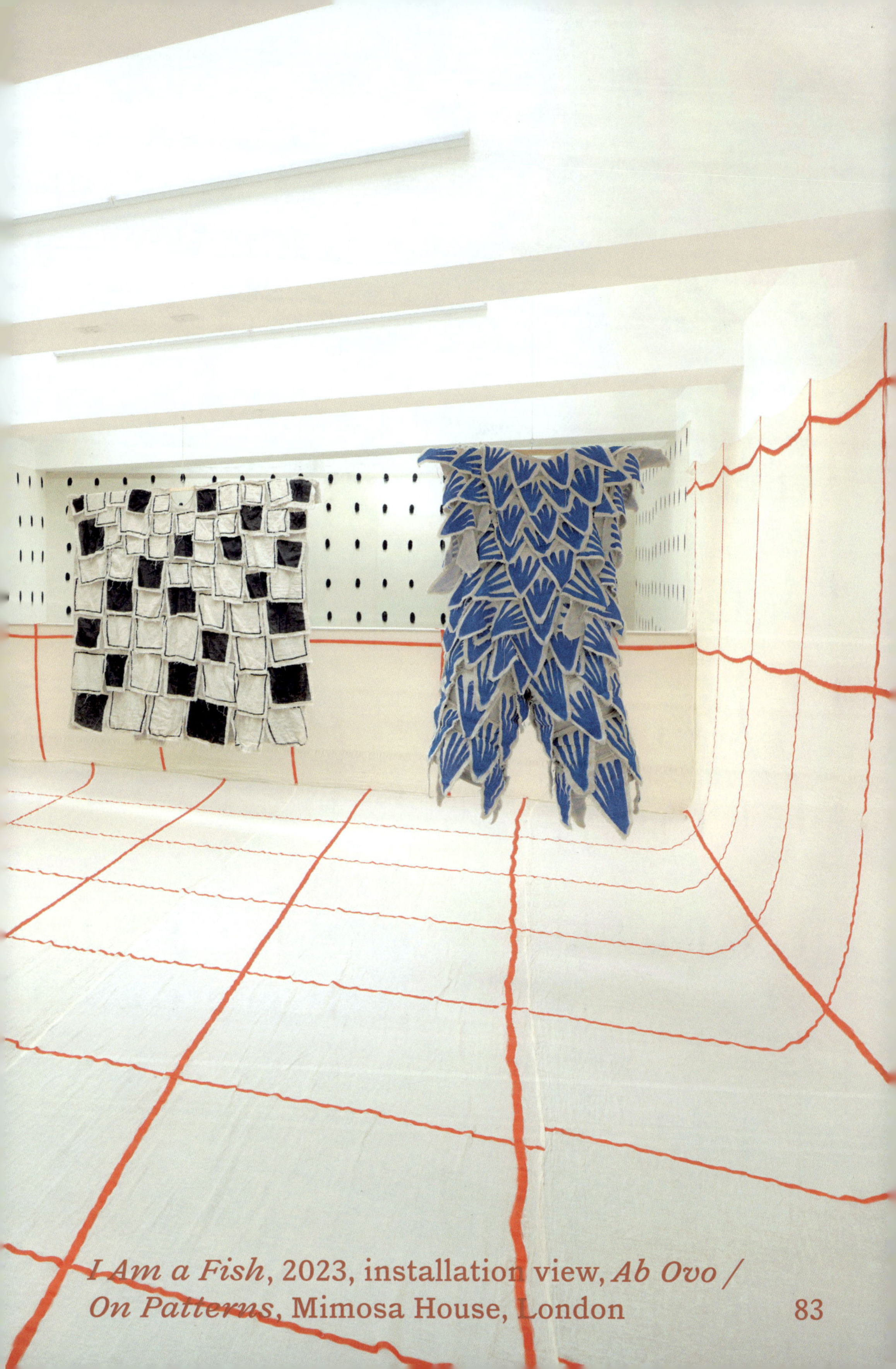

I Am a Fish, 2023, installation view, *Ab Ovo / On Patterns*, Mimosa House, London

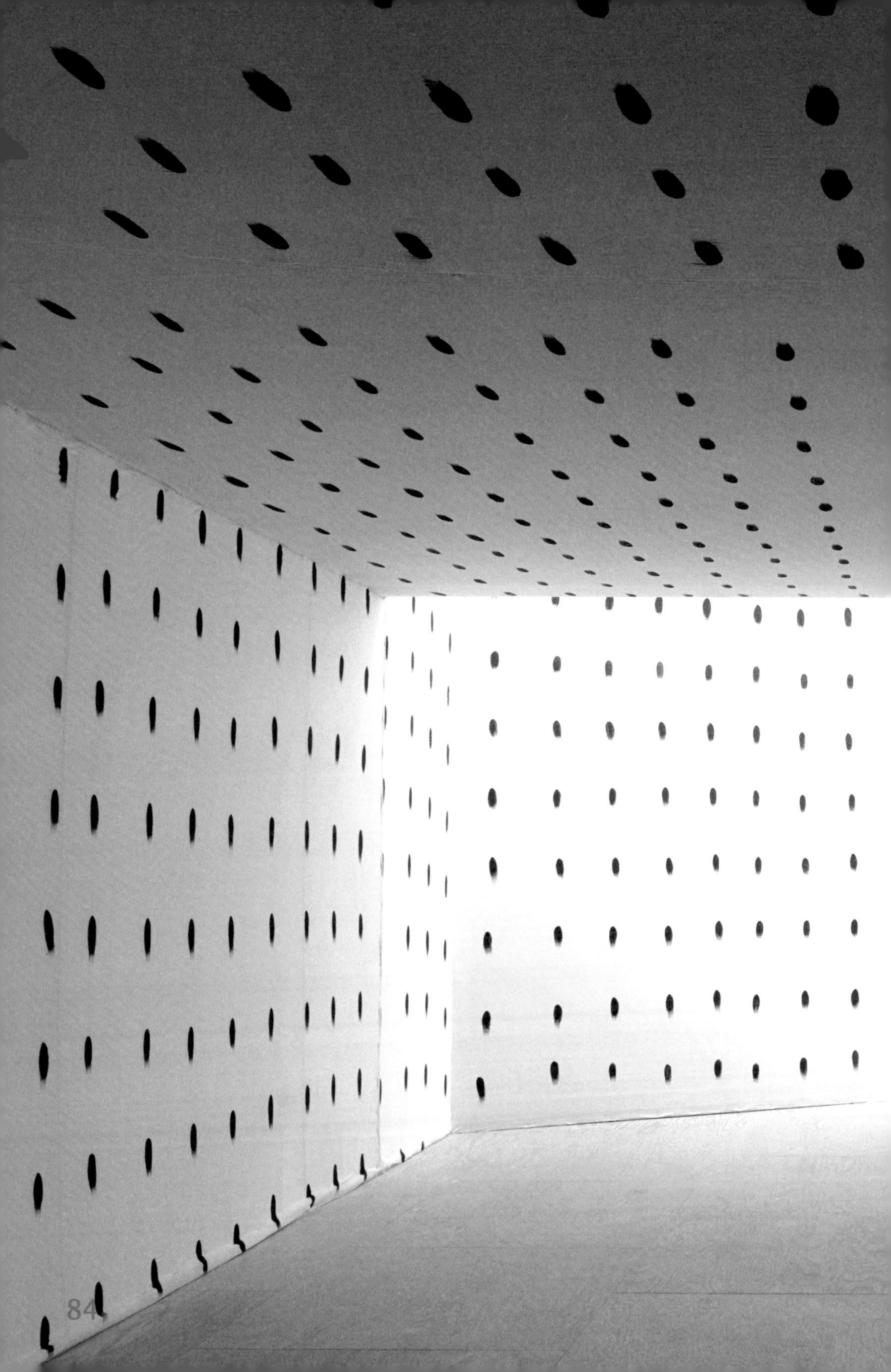

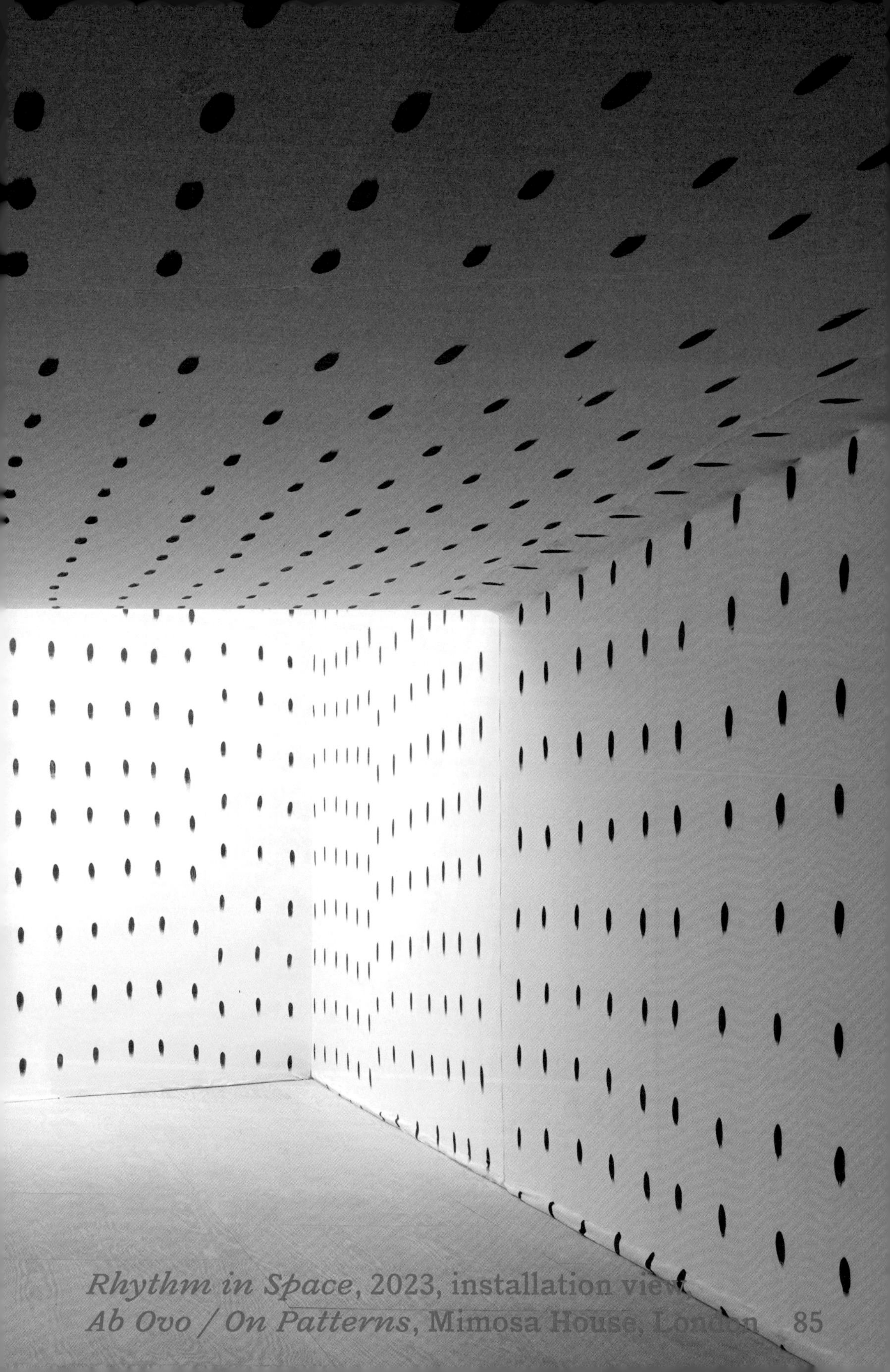

Rhythm in Space, 2023, installation view,
Ab Ovo / On Patterns, Mimosa House, London

This is what is worth doing for me now: stripes, circles, squares, triangles, modules, large drawings that one can wear. I am looking for an opening to flow out, beyond painting. A point where drawing can go into the three dimensions, but not in stone, not in iron, not in bronze. It's not sculpture, it's space.

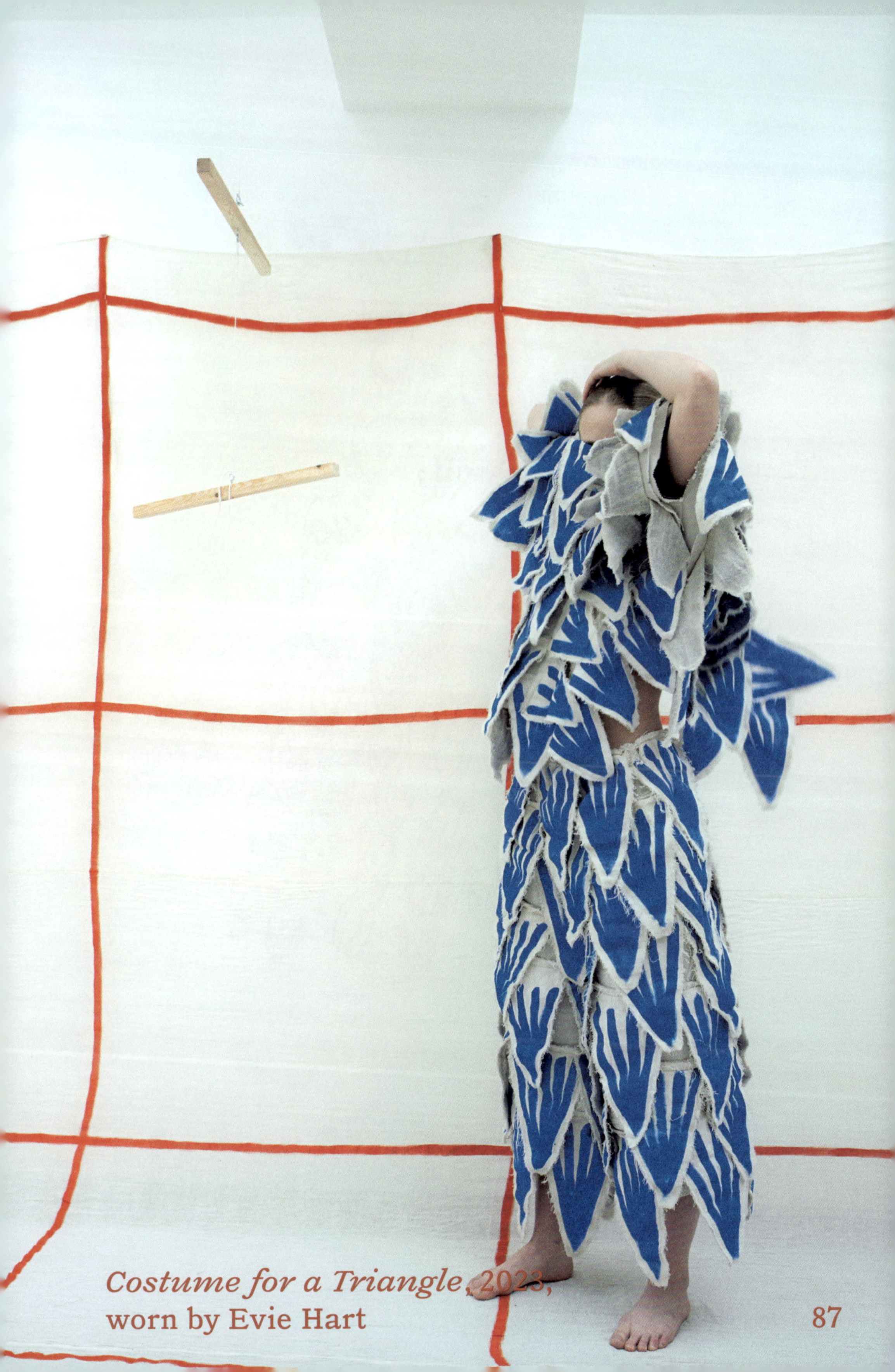

Costume for a Triangle, 2023,
worn by Evie Hart

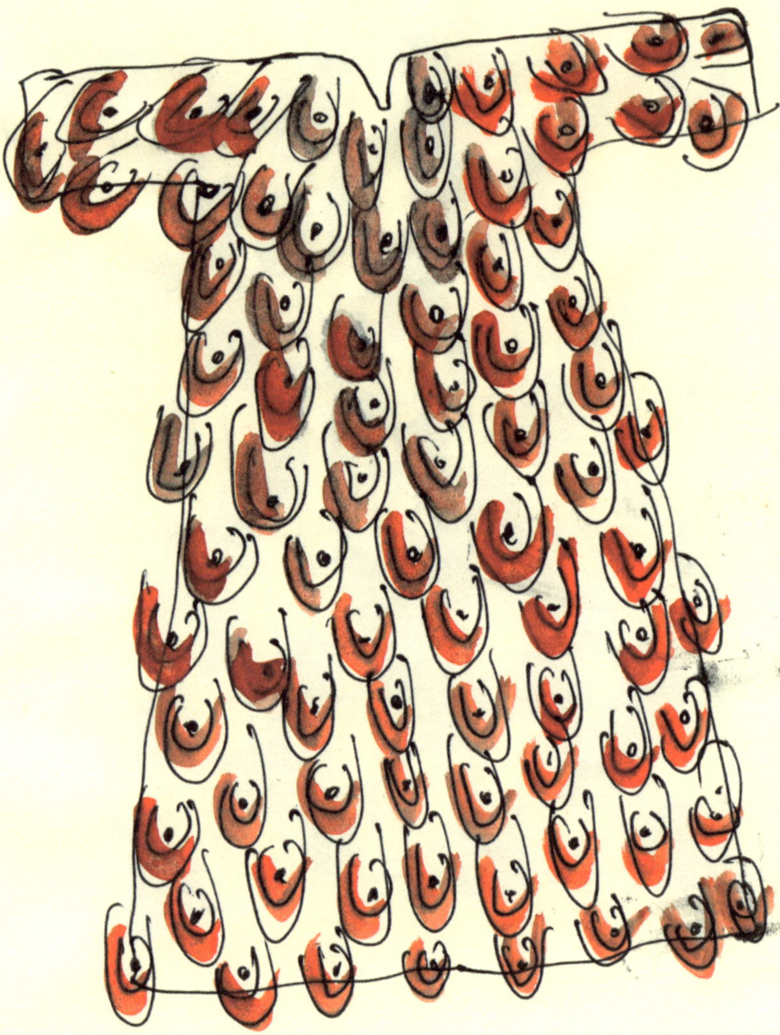

Sketch for Costume for a Circle, 2022, gouache and ink on paper, 25 × 19 cm

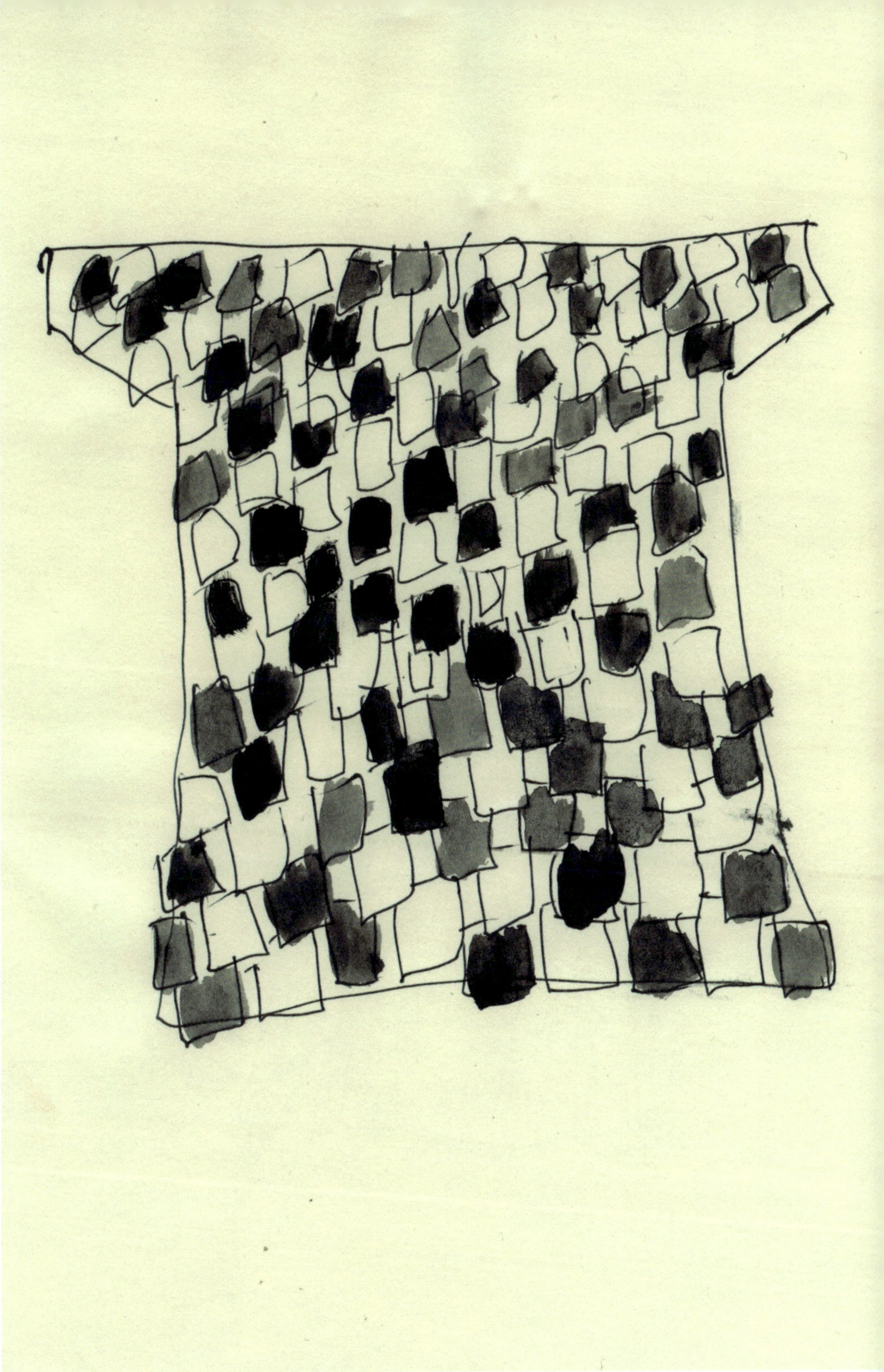

Sketch for Costume for a Square, 2022, gouache and ink on paper, 25 × 19 cm

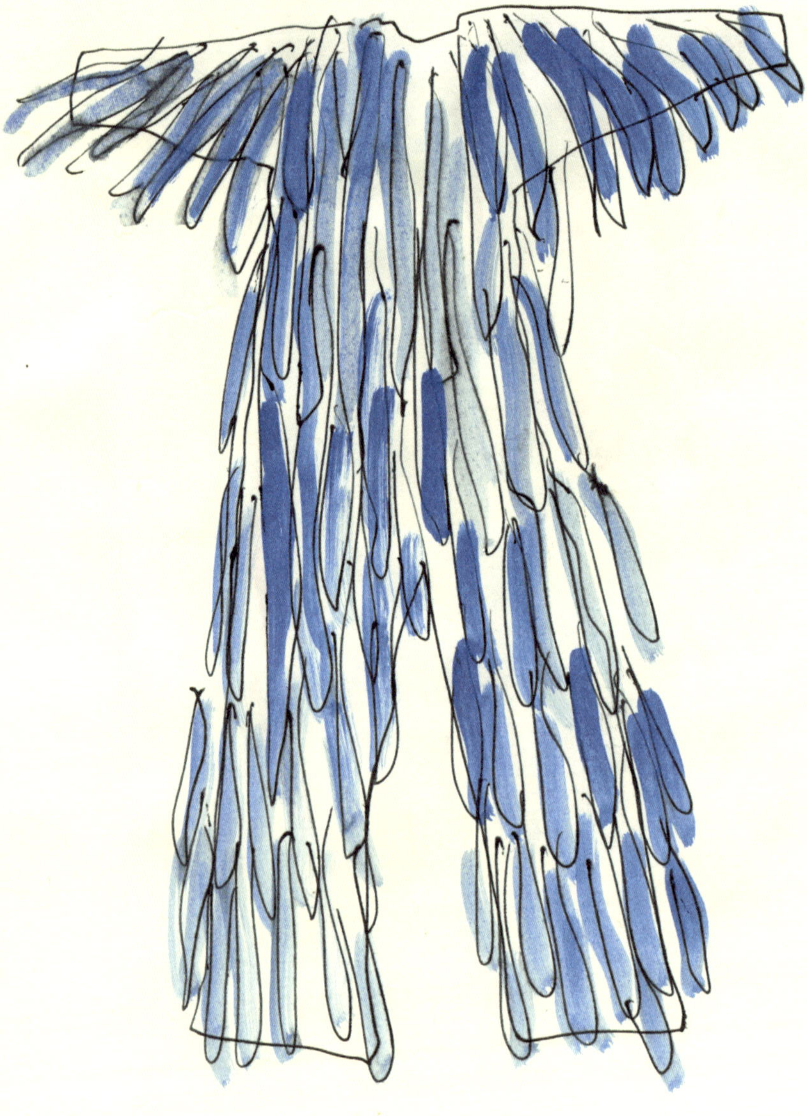

Sketch for Costume for a Triangle, 2022,
gouache and ink on paper, 25 × 19 cm

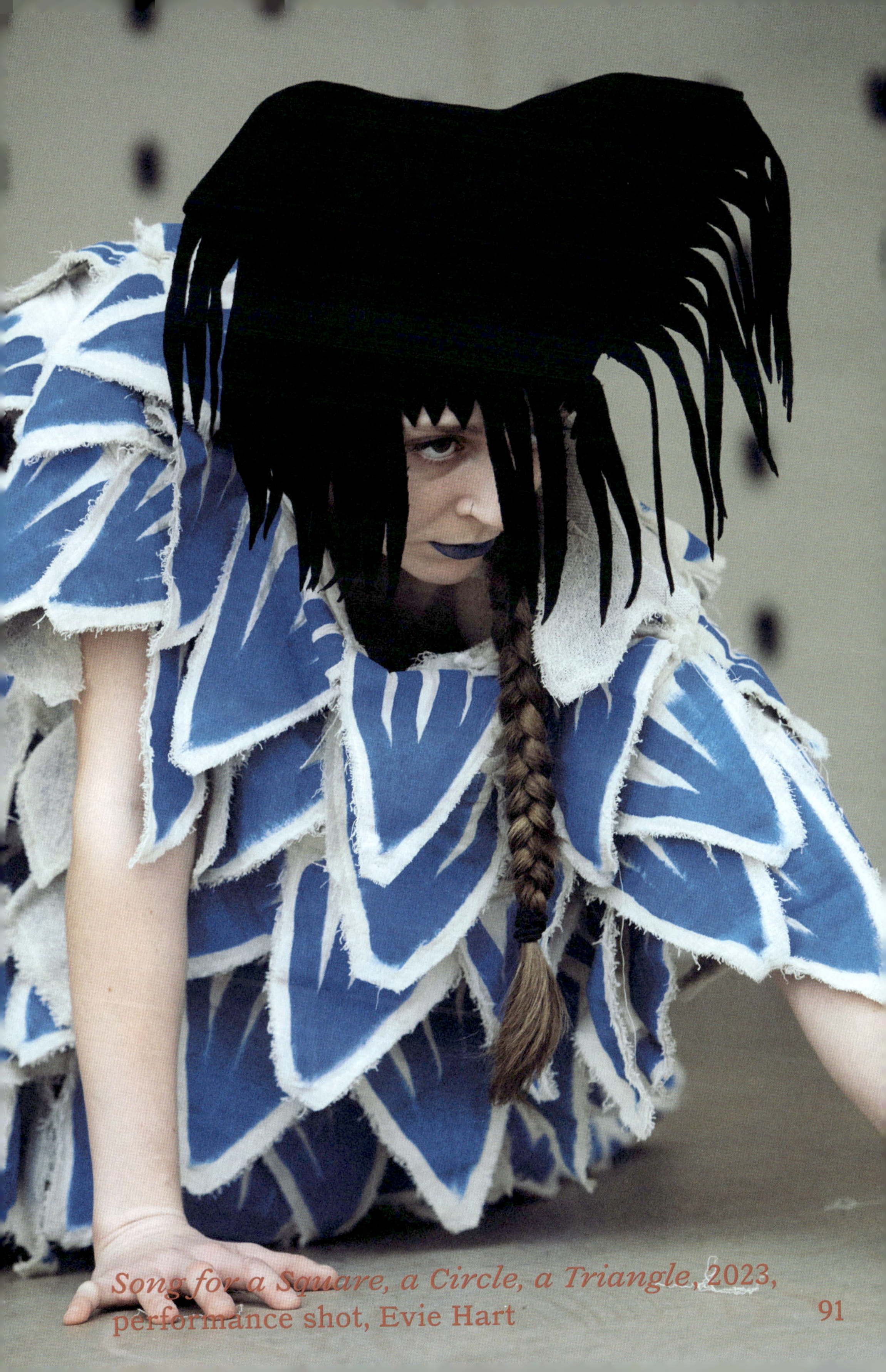

Song for a Square, a Circle, a Triangle, 2023, performance shot, Evie Hart

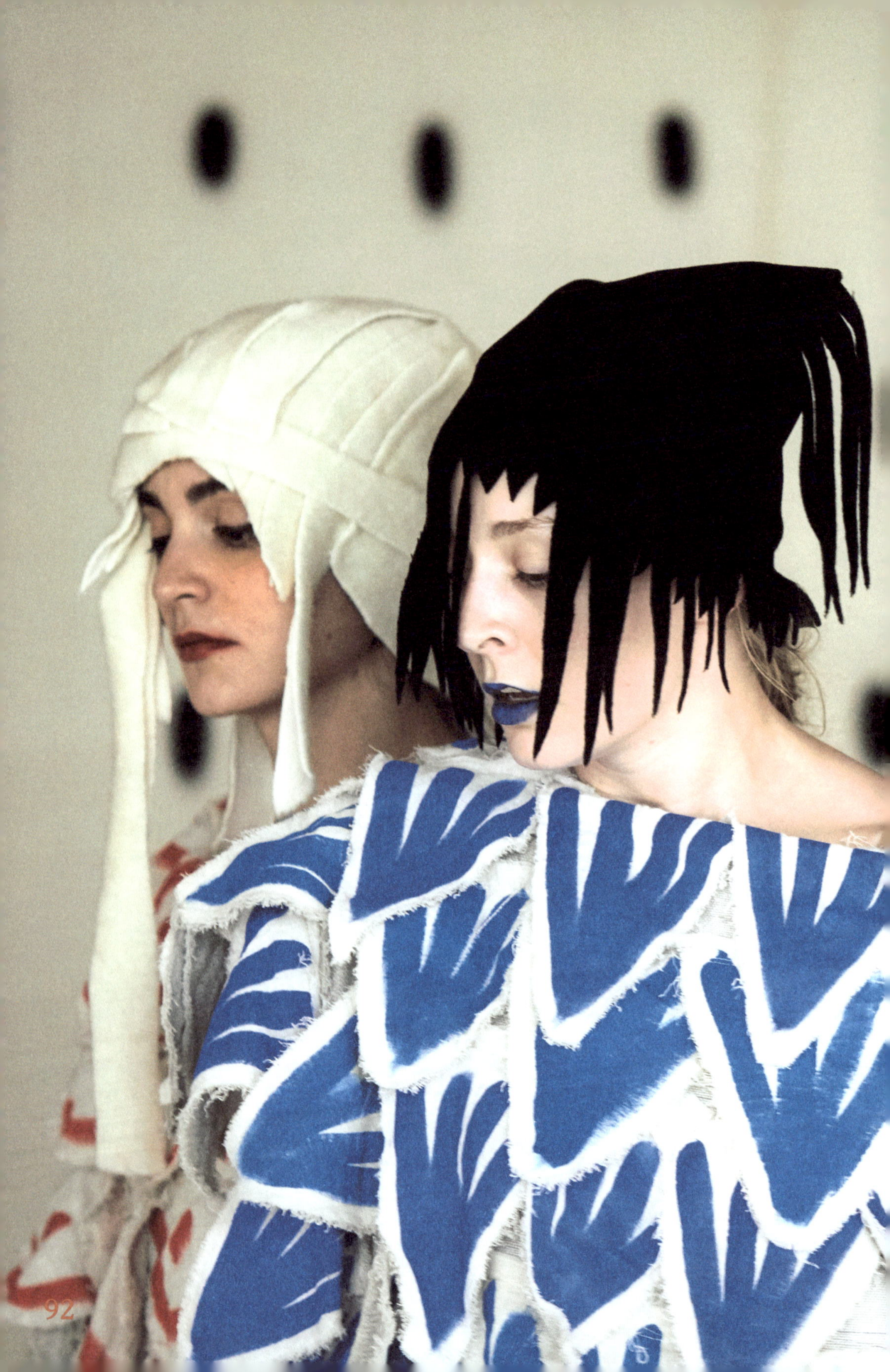

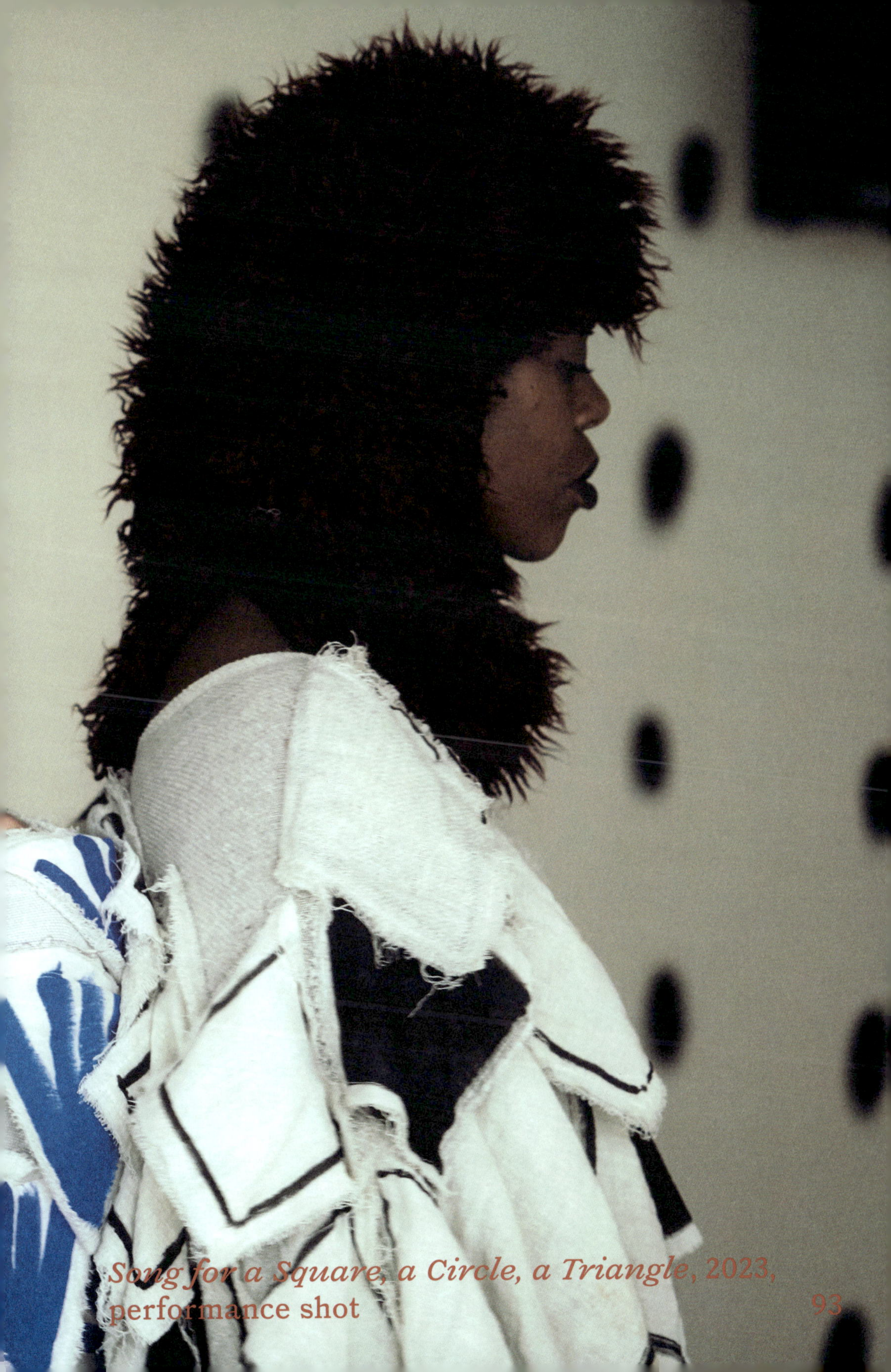

Song for a Square, a Circle, a Triangle, 2023,
performance shot

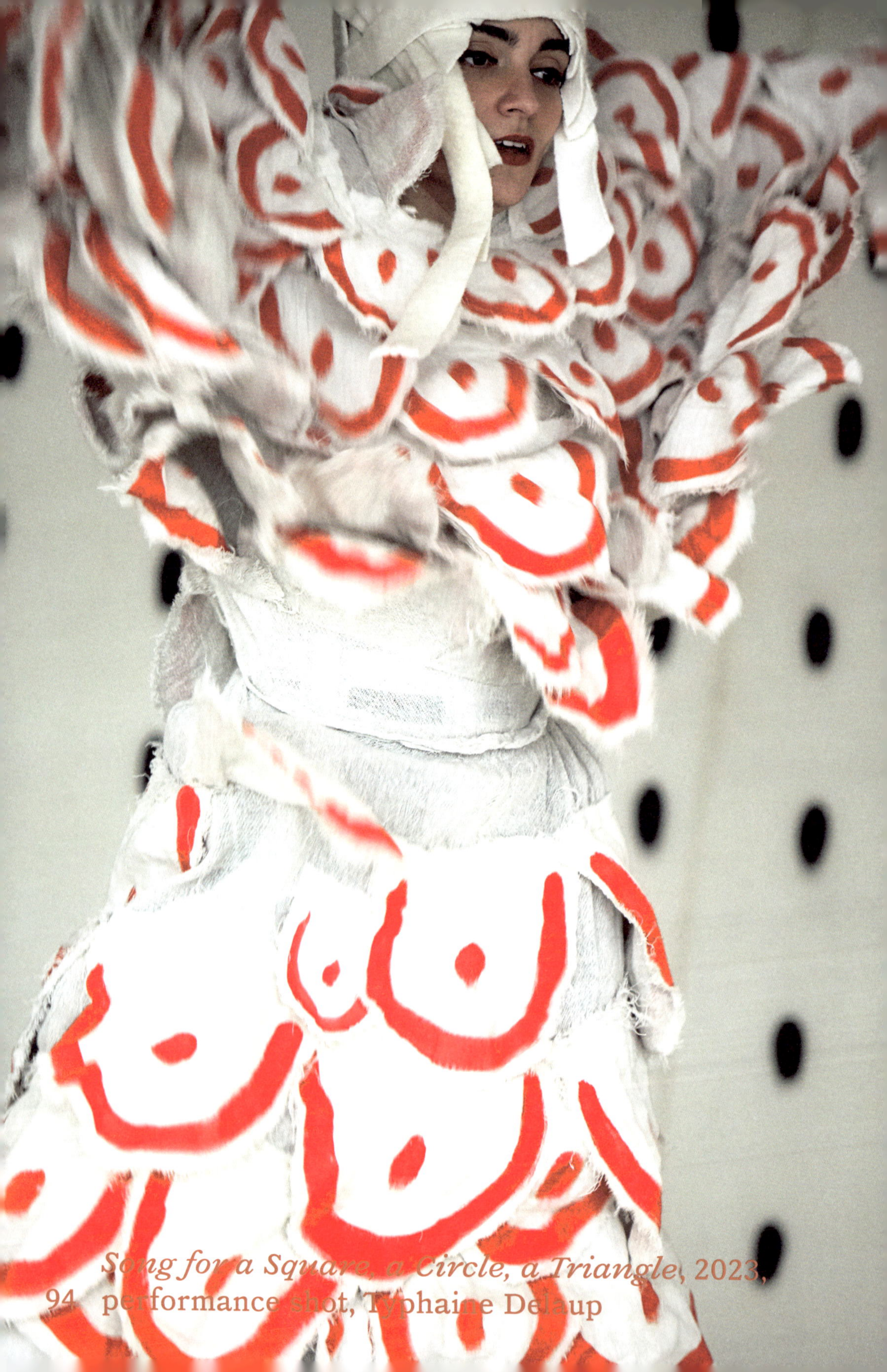

Song for a Square, a Circle, a Triangle, 2023,
performance shot, Typhaine Delaup

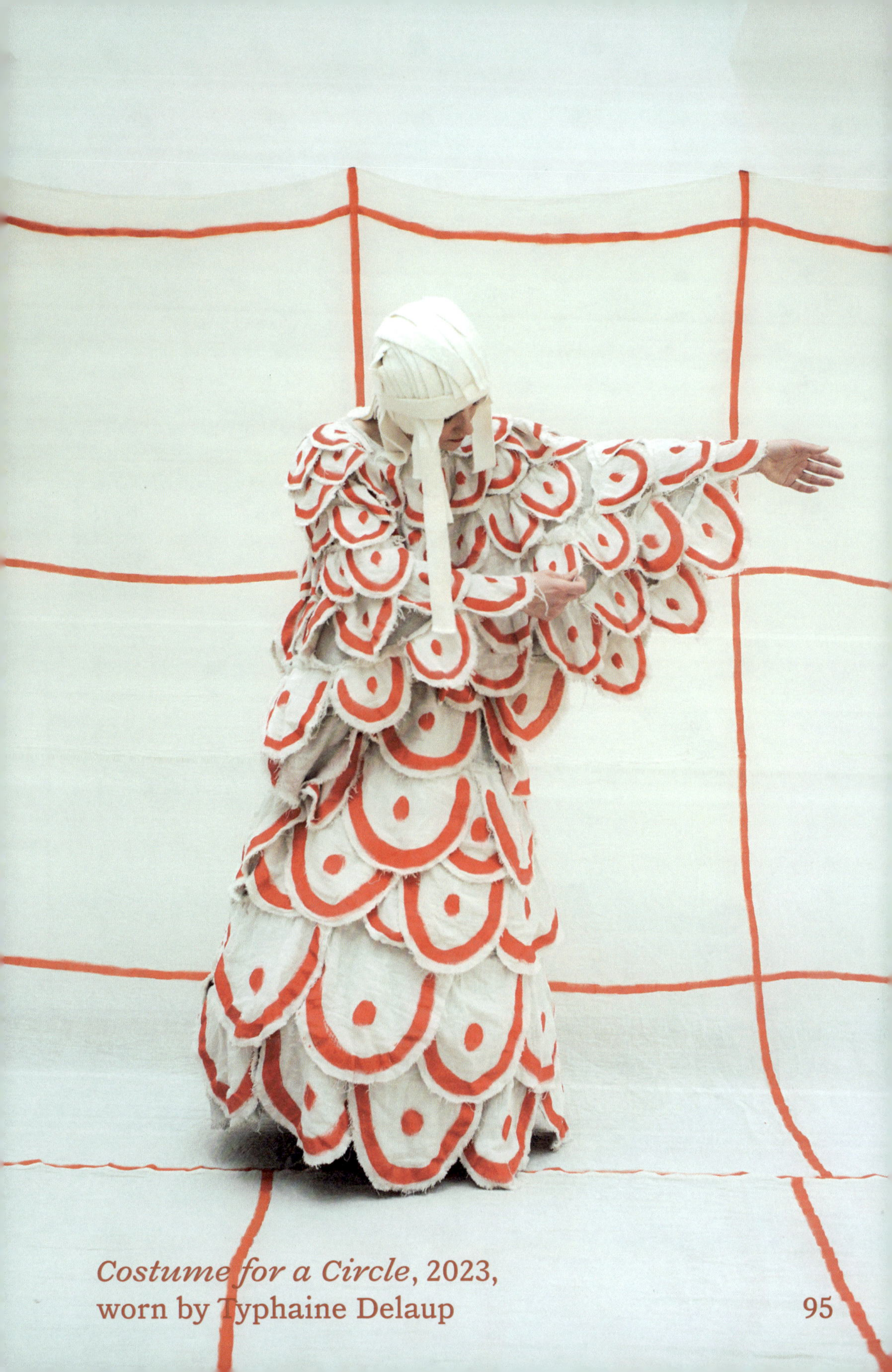

Costume for a Circle, 2023,
worn by Typhaine Delaup

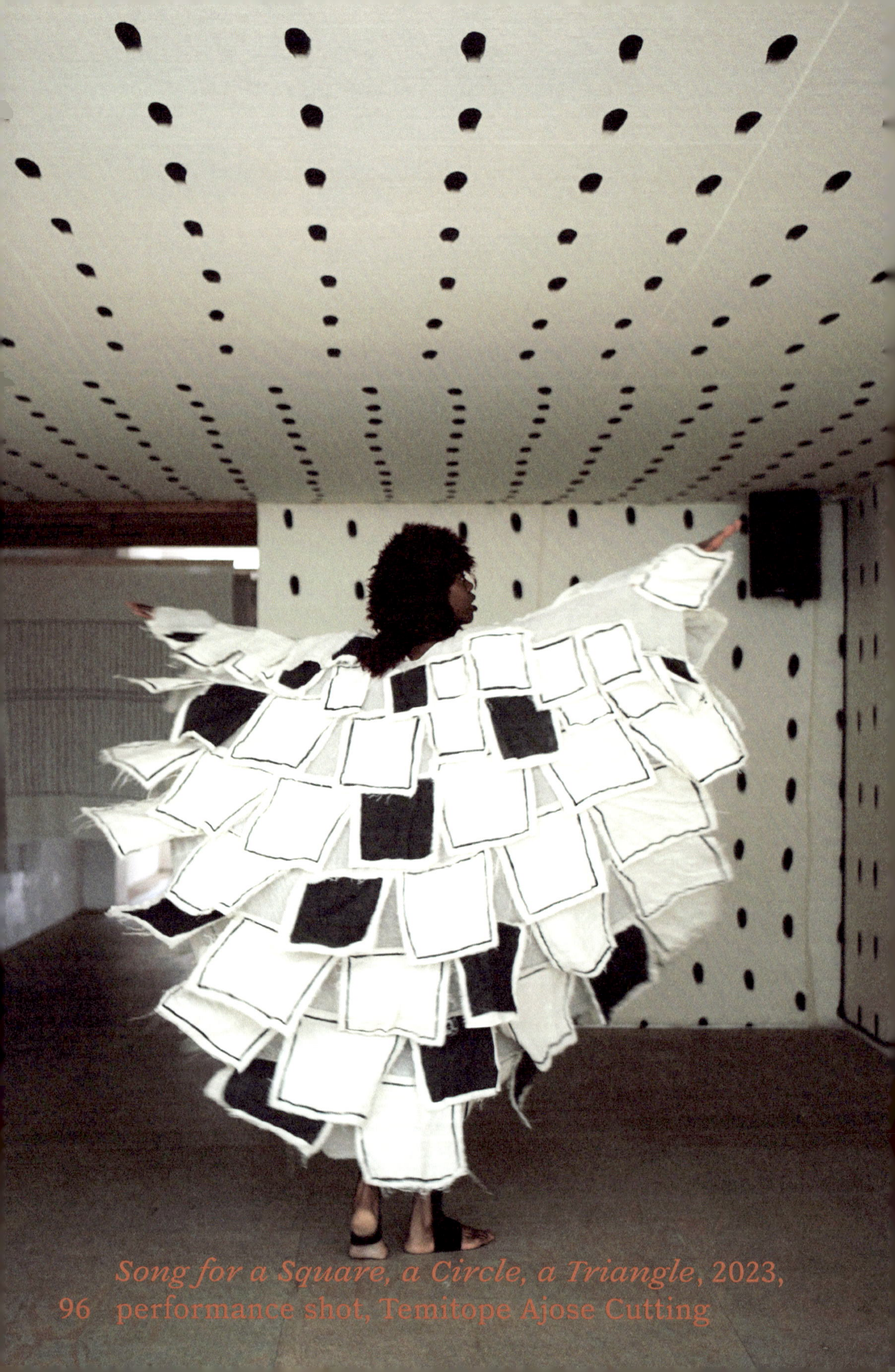

Song for a Square, a Circle, a Triangle, 2023,
performance shot, Temitope Ajose Cutting

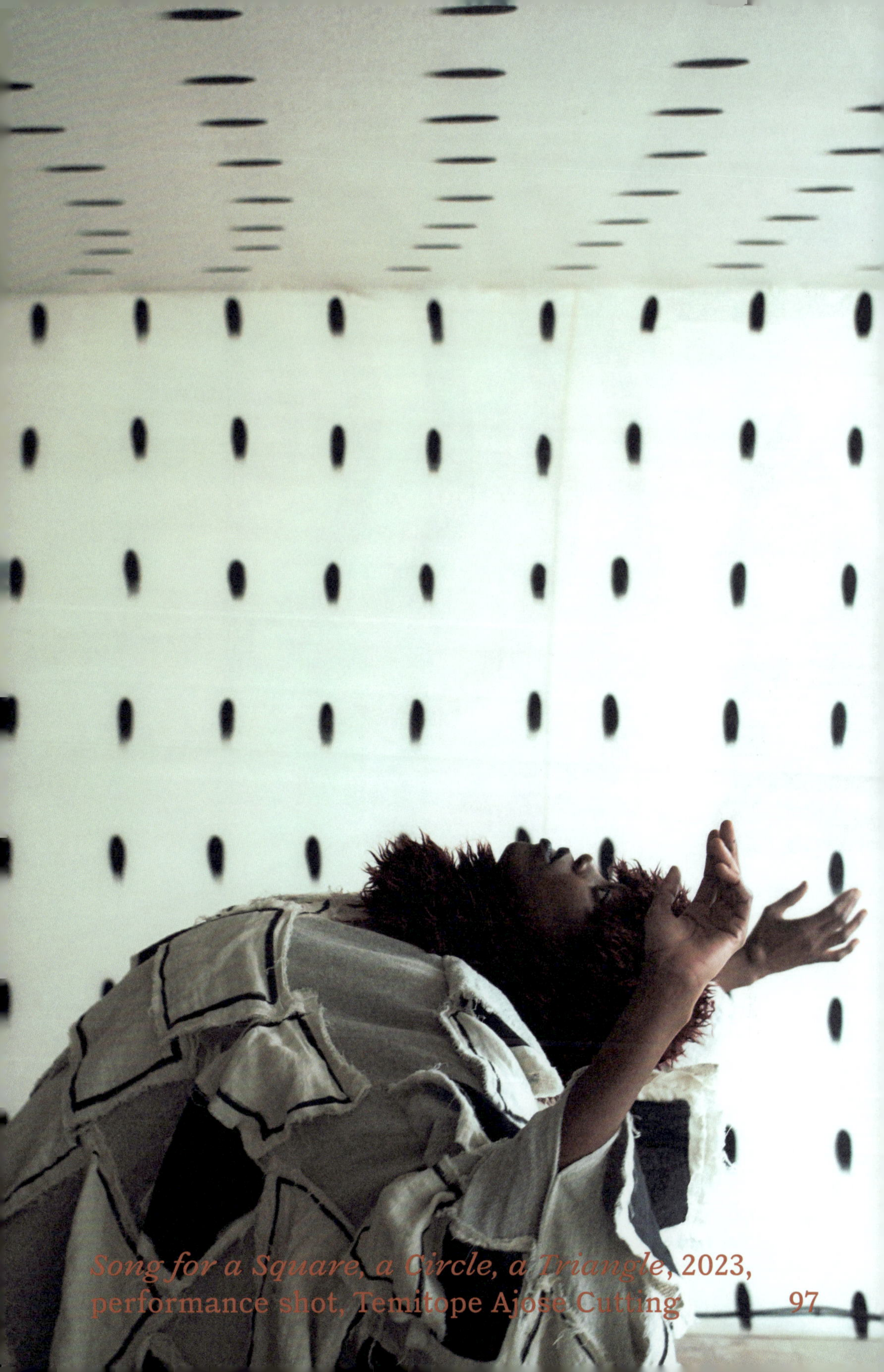

Song for a Square, a Circle, a Triangle, 2023, performance shot, Temitope Ajose Cutting

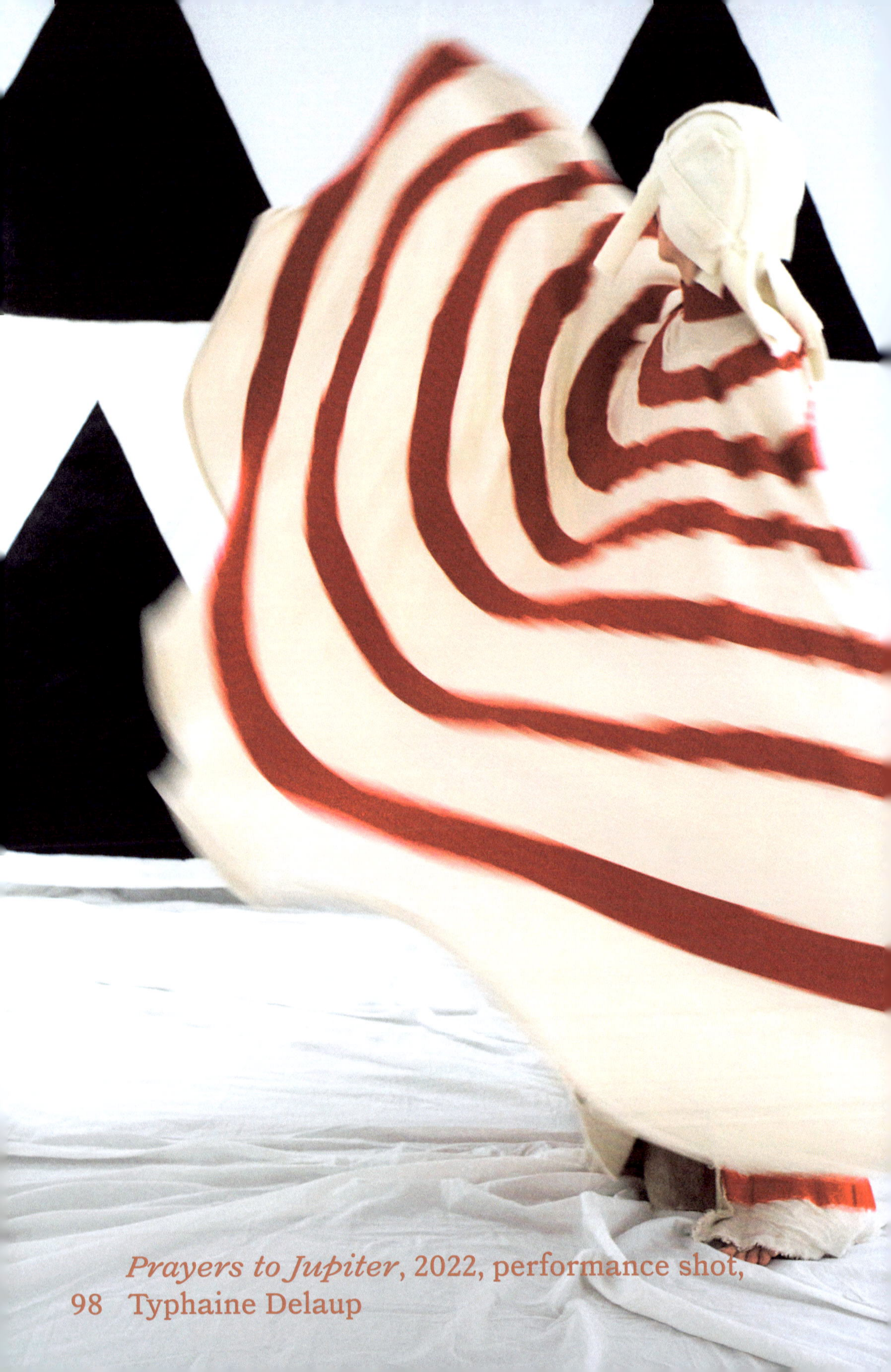

Prayers to Jupiter, 2022, performance shot,
Typhaine Delaup

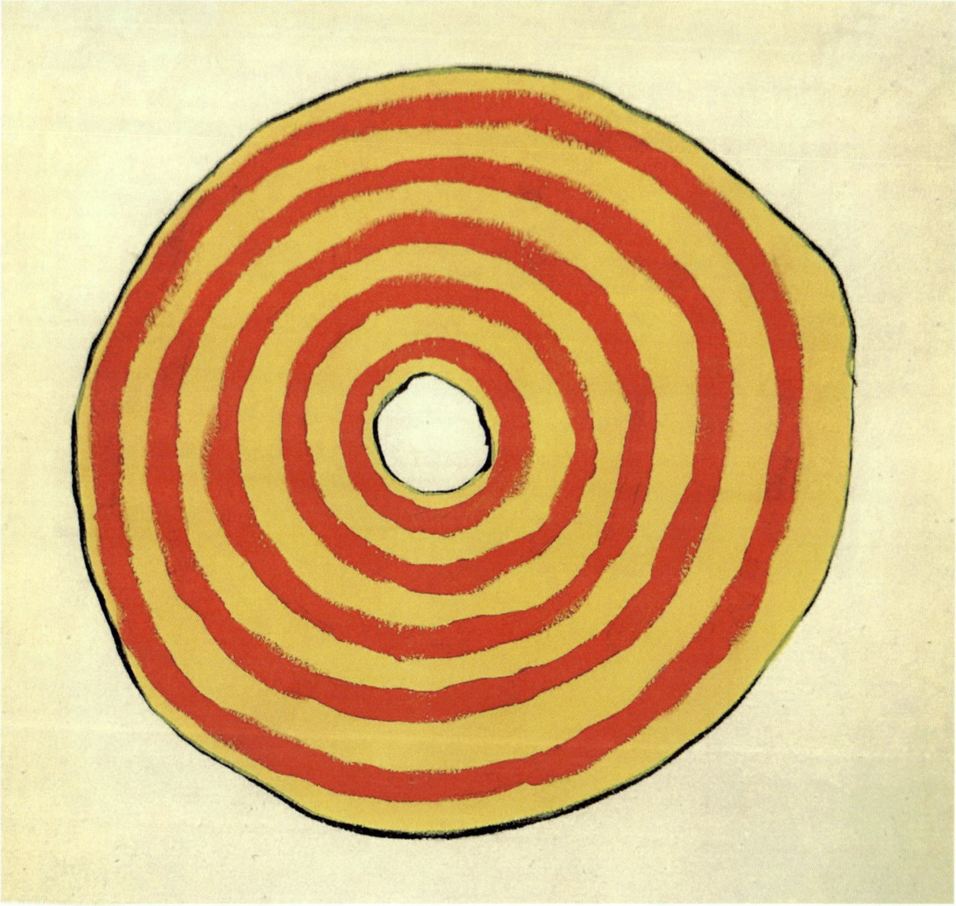

Sketch for the Costume for Prayers to Jupiter,
2022, vinyl paint on paper, detail

When you think of the universe . . . you think, OK, we are on Earth, which is in the Solar System, the Solar System is in the Milky Way which is our galaxy, all around it are other galaxies, and beyond those? What's beyond all this? Where does space end? What does it all rest upon? The idea of infinity is a true vertigo. And I think we deal with this vertigo with geometry and with abstract decorative patterns.

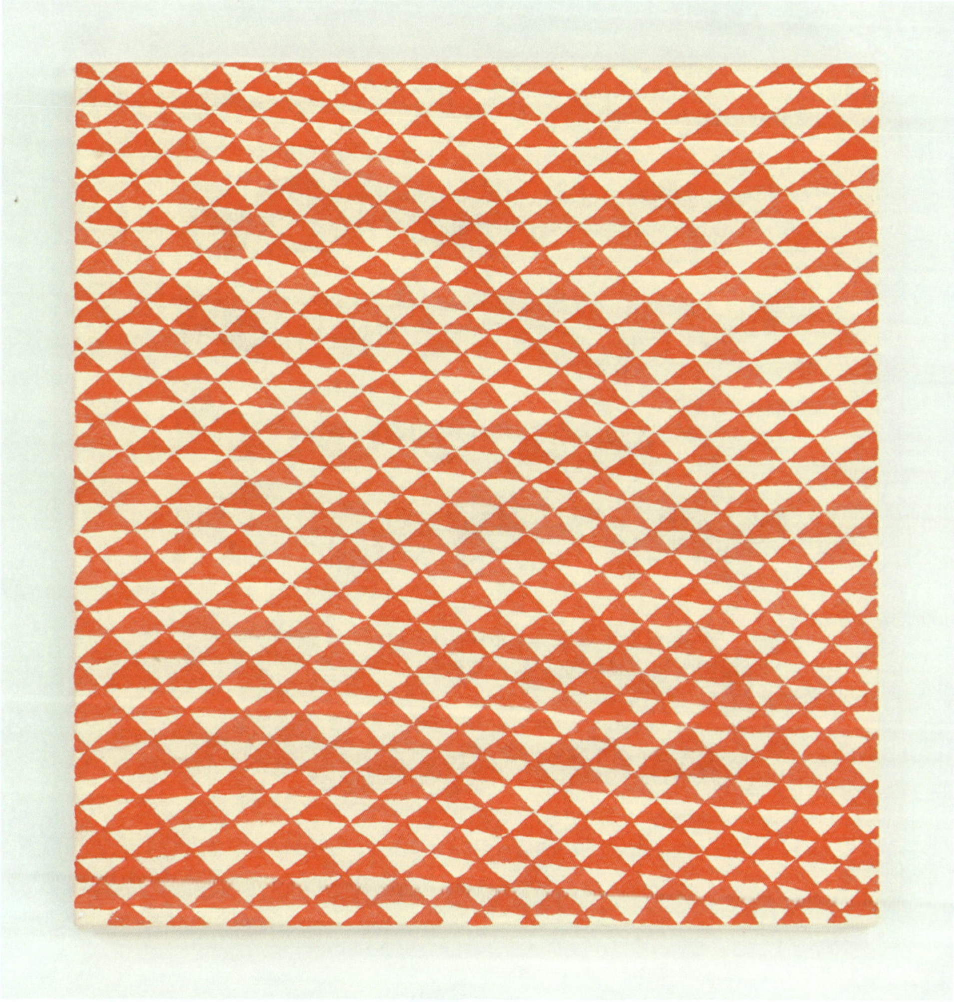

Drawings for Myself. Red Triangles, 2021,
vinyl paint and pencil on canvas, 35 × 34 cm

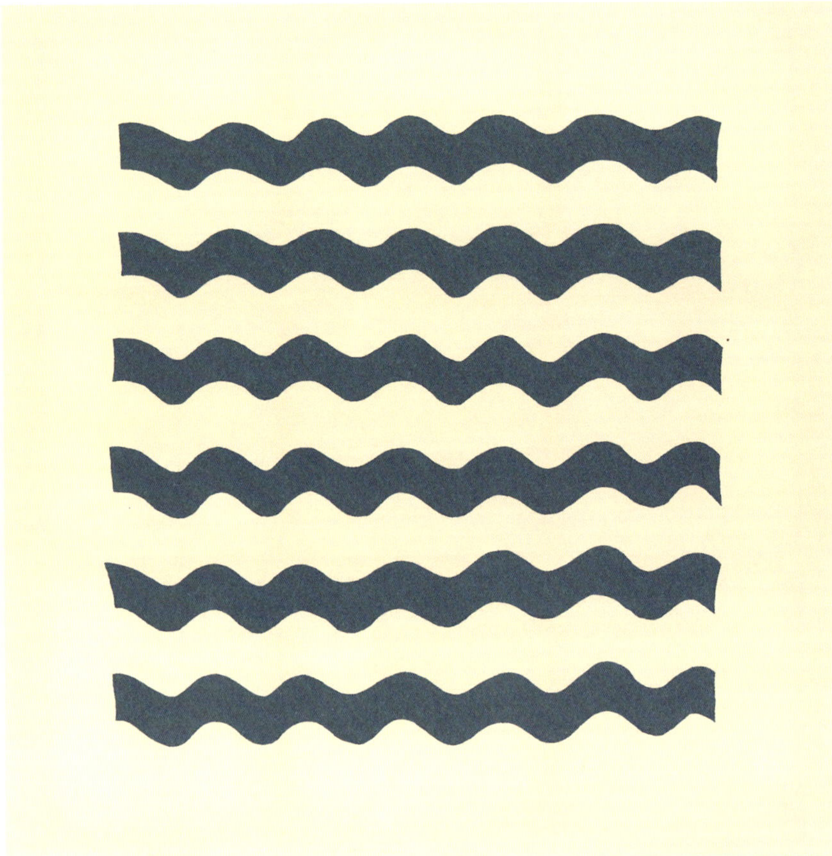

102 *Il mare*, 2019, wool stitched on flannel, 210 × 210 cm

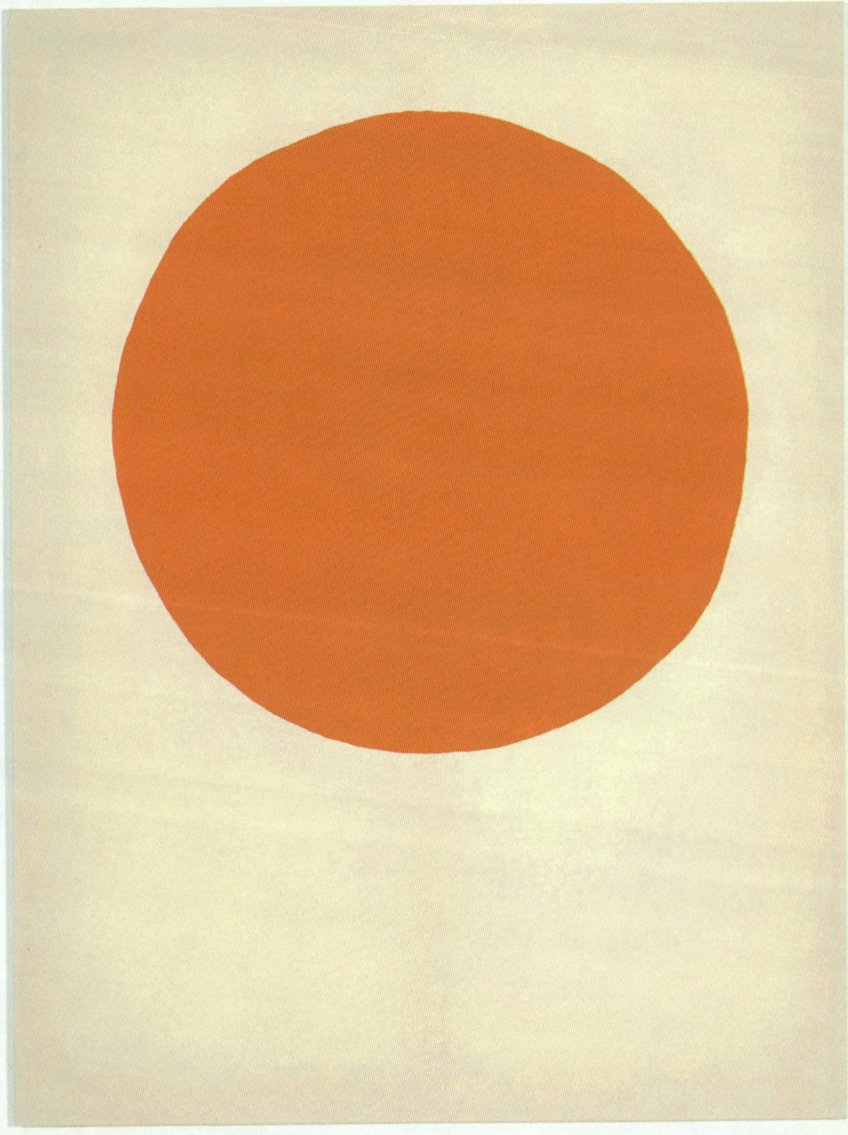

Il sole, 2019, wool stitched on canvas, 240 × 184 cm

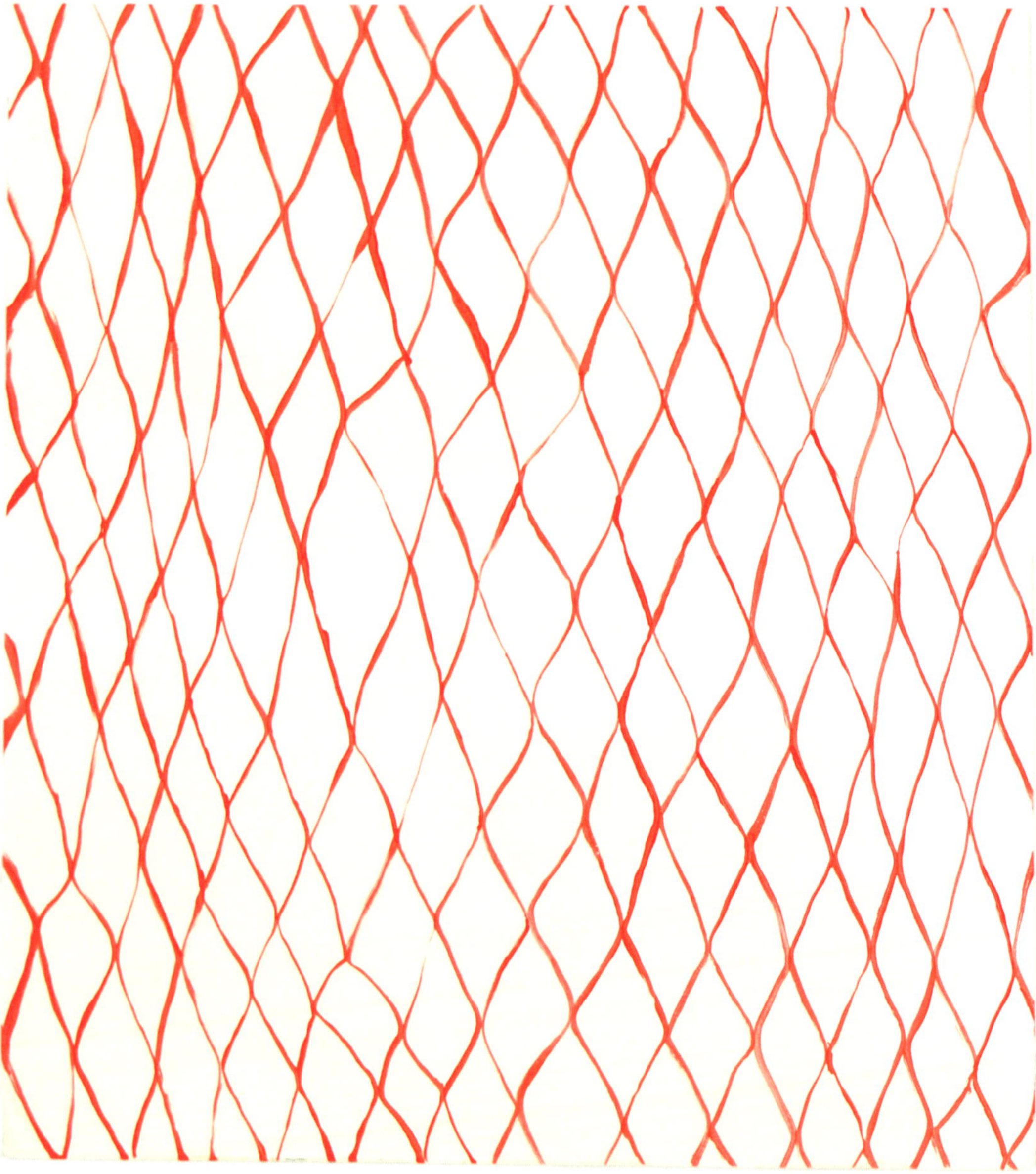

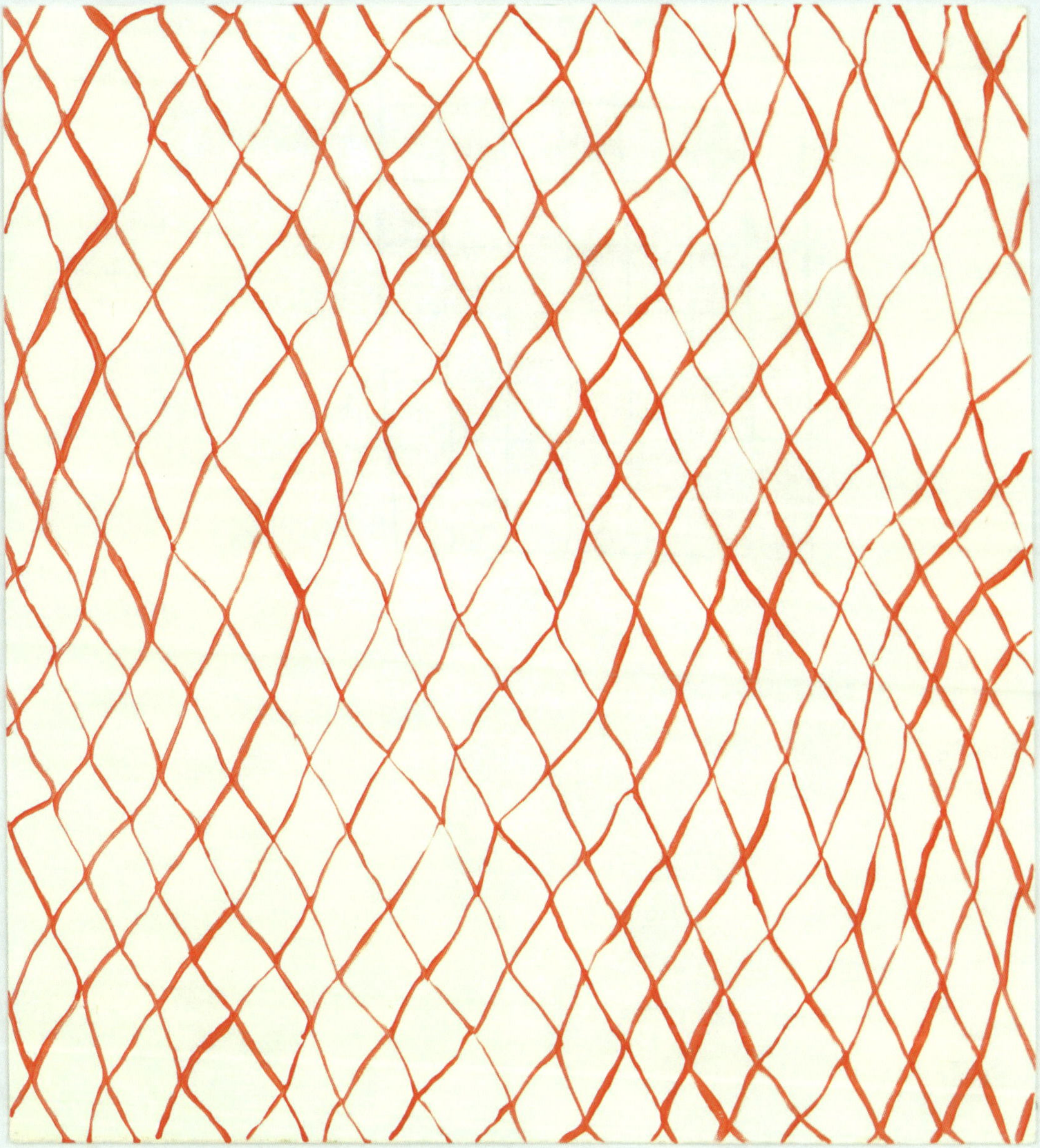

I Am a Fish, 2019, vinyl paint on board, dyptych, each 38 × 35 cm

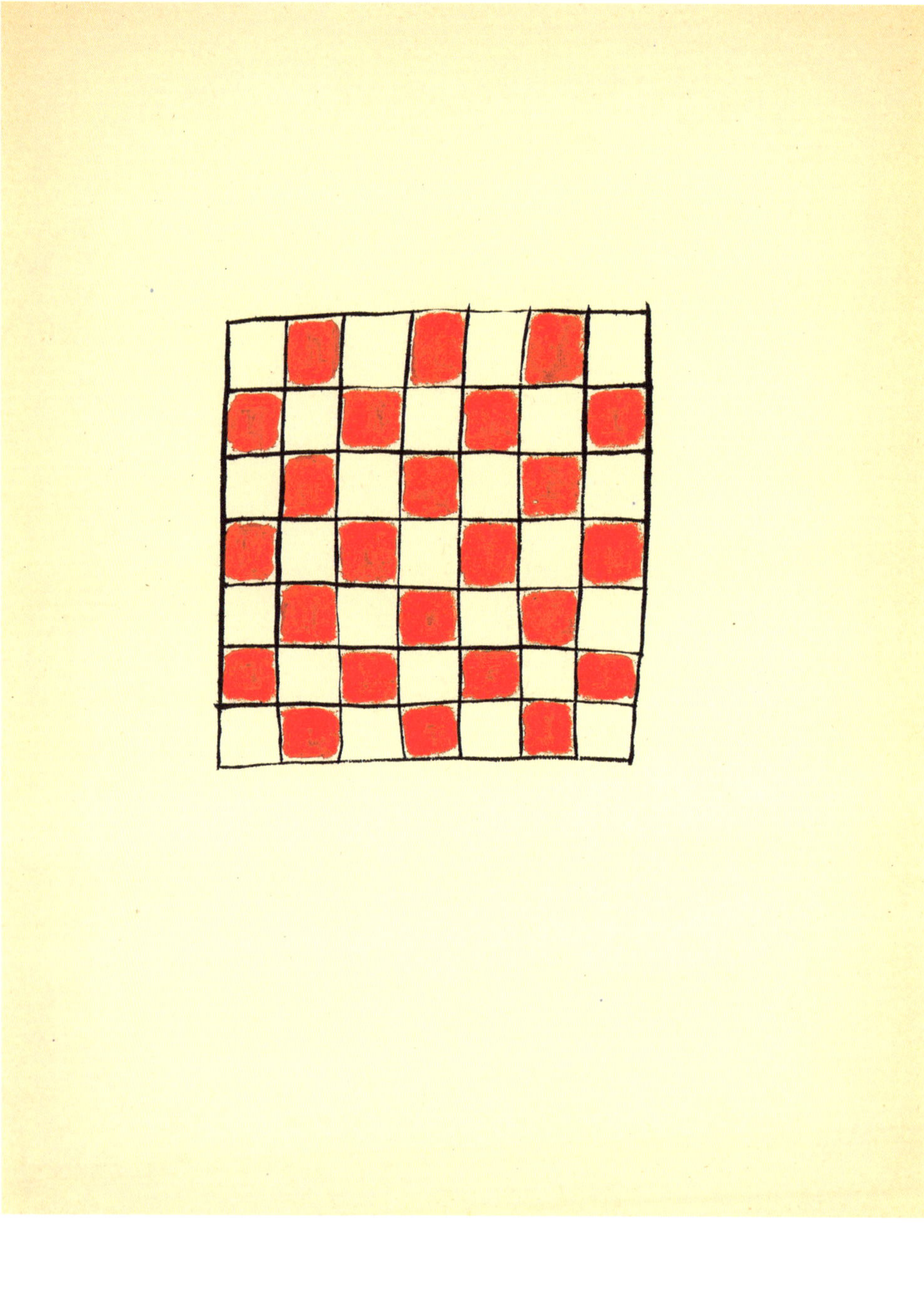

Scacchiera inutilizzabile rossa, 2019, vinyl paint and Indian ink on paper, 28 × 22 cm

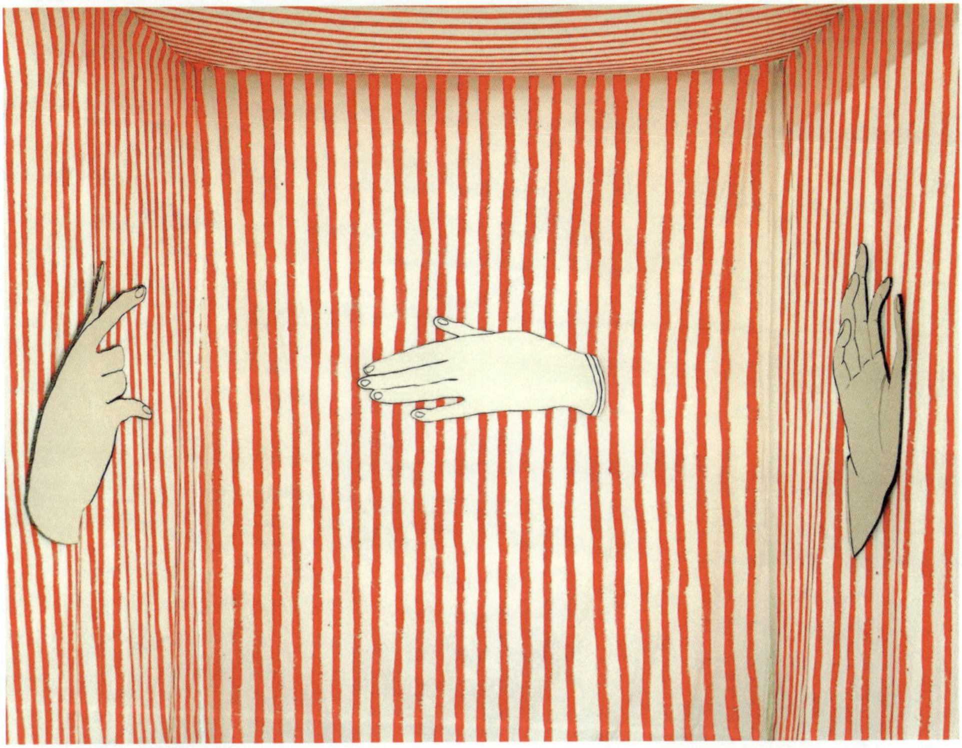

Six or Seven (Is the Number of Times Mary Speaks), 2020, detail of the installation

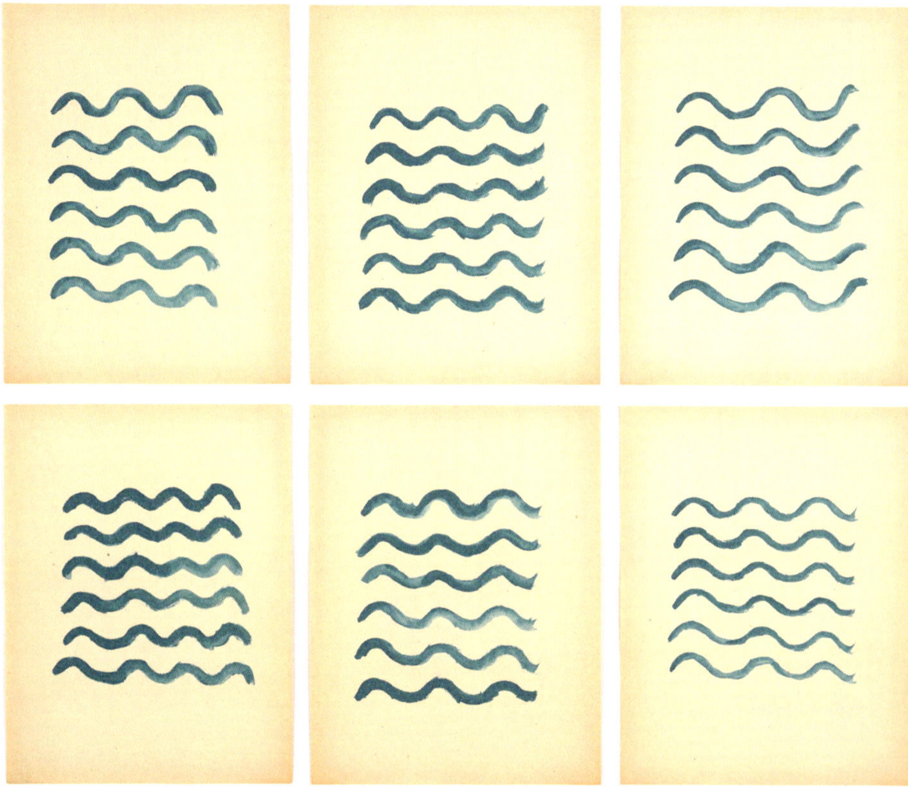

Sketches for Il Mare, 2019, vinyl paint on paper, 6 pages, each 28 × 22 cm

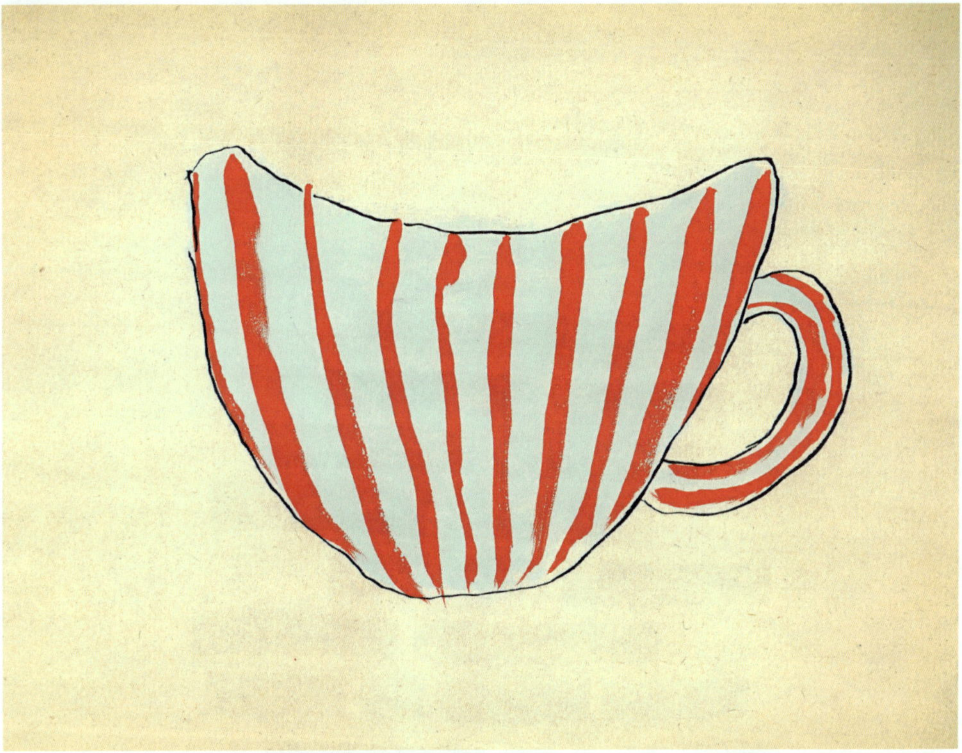

Drawings for Myself. Blue Cup, 2020, vinyl paint and Indian ink on paper, 22 × 28 cm

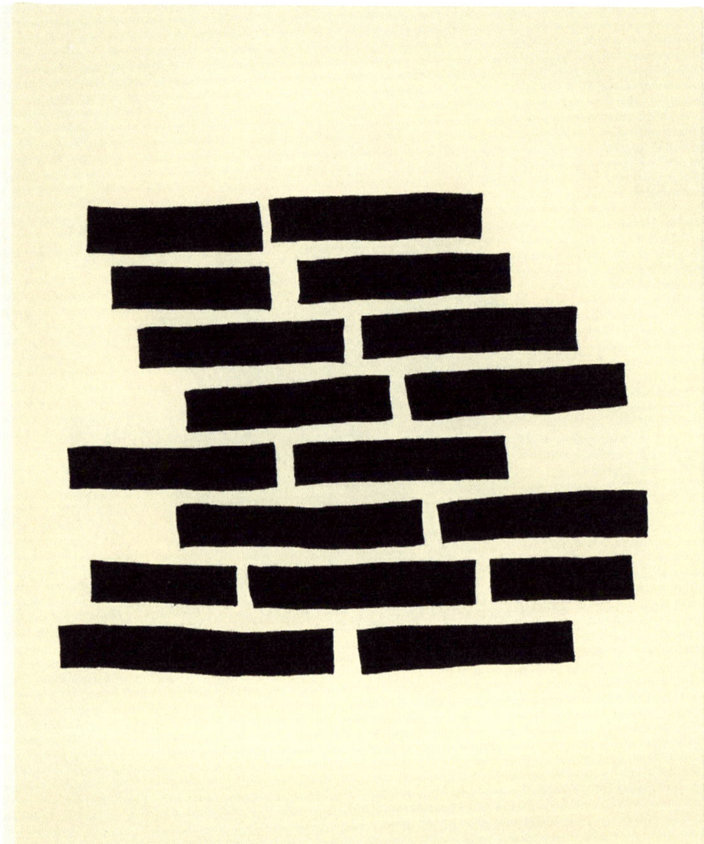

Ab Ovo. Black Pattern, 2020, wool stitched on canvas, 88 × 74 cm

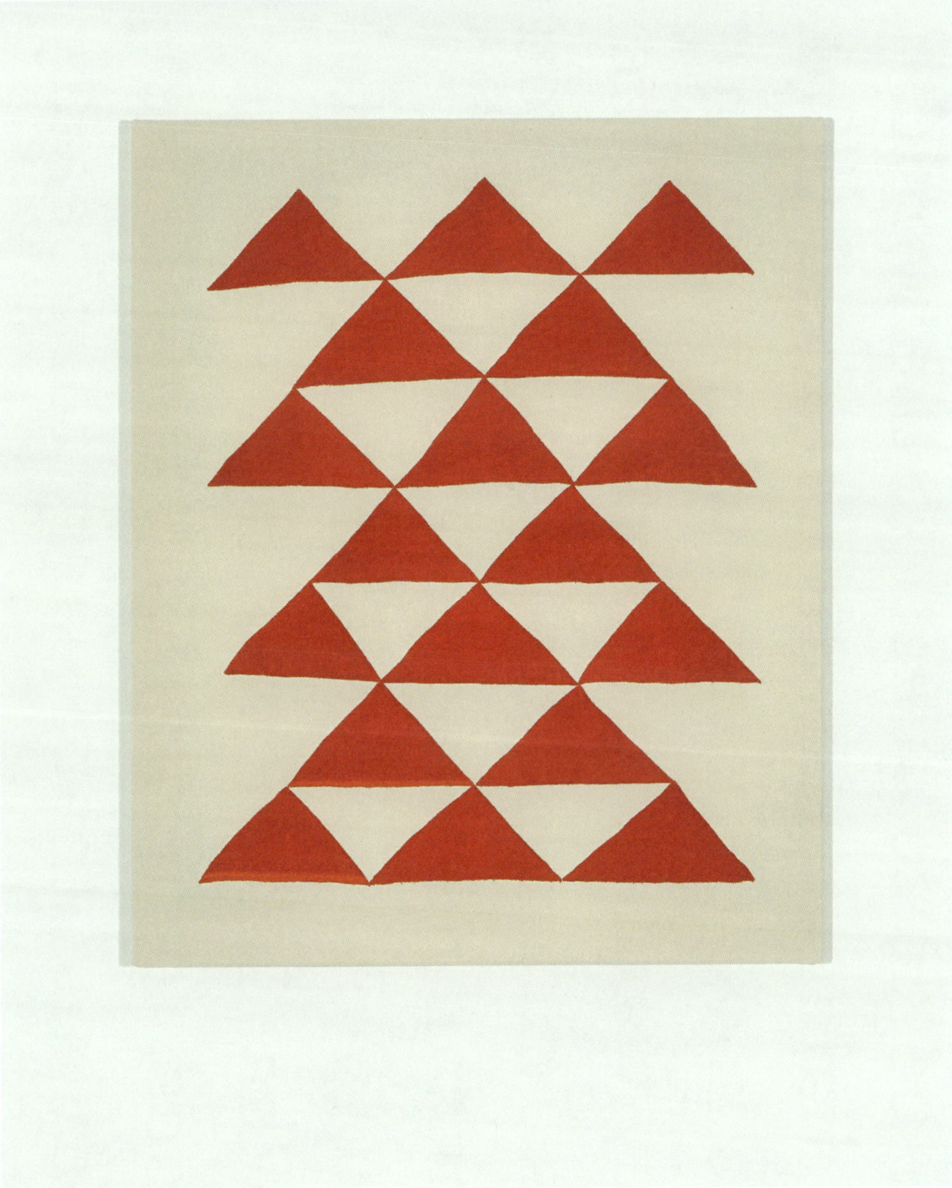

Ab Ovo. Red Pattern, 2020, fabric stitched on canvas, 88 × 74 cm

When we begin to question the world our first dialogue is with nature. I think all artists have a fixation with it, even when they wanted to destroy it like the Futurists. Nature is the beauty that you know you can never grasp whole, the game you know you're always going to lose at. What I do now is try to imitate its methods, to think that I am nature in my body and that I carry that beauty in my organs.

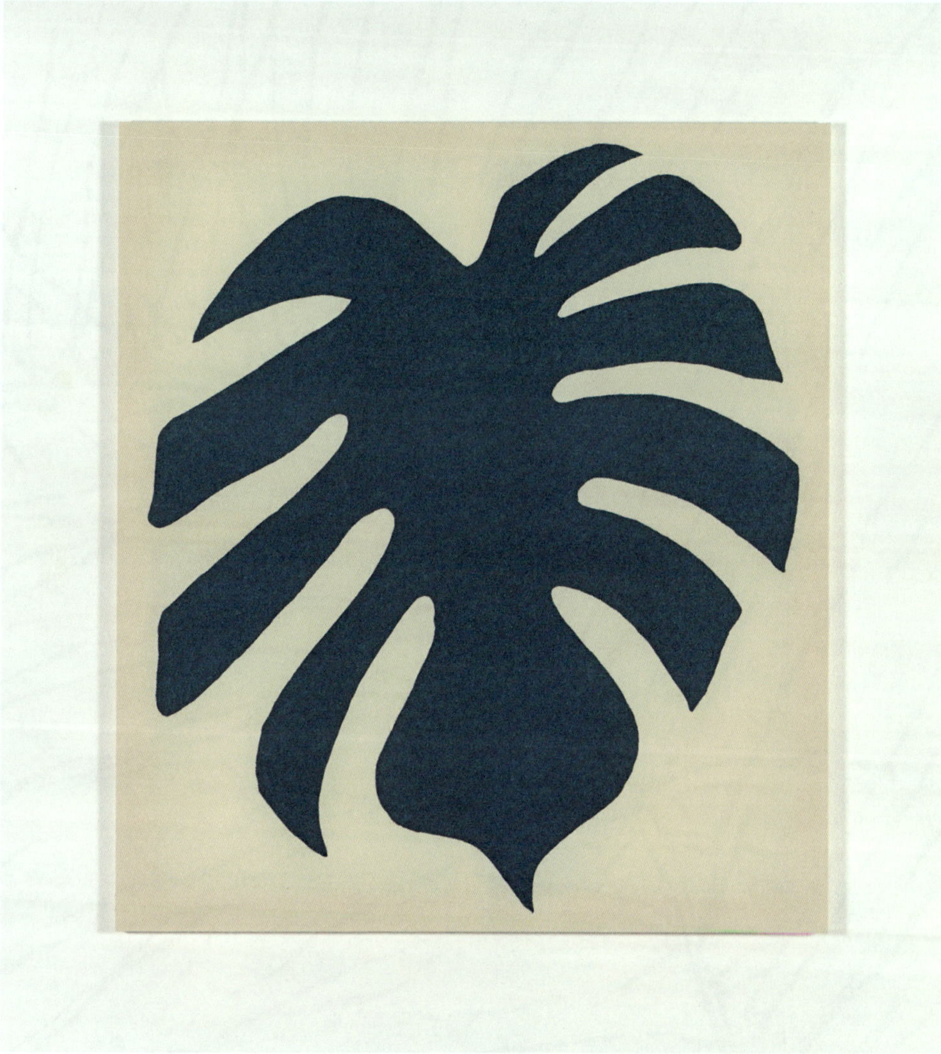

Ab Ovo. Green Leaf, 2020, wool stitched on canvas, 140 × 129 cm

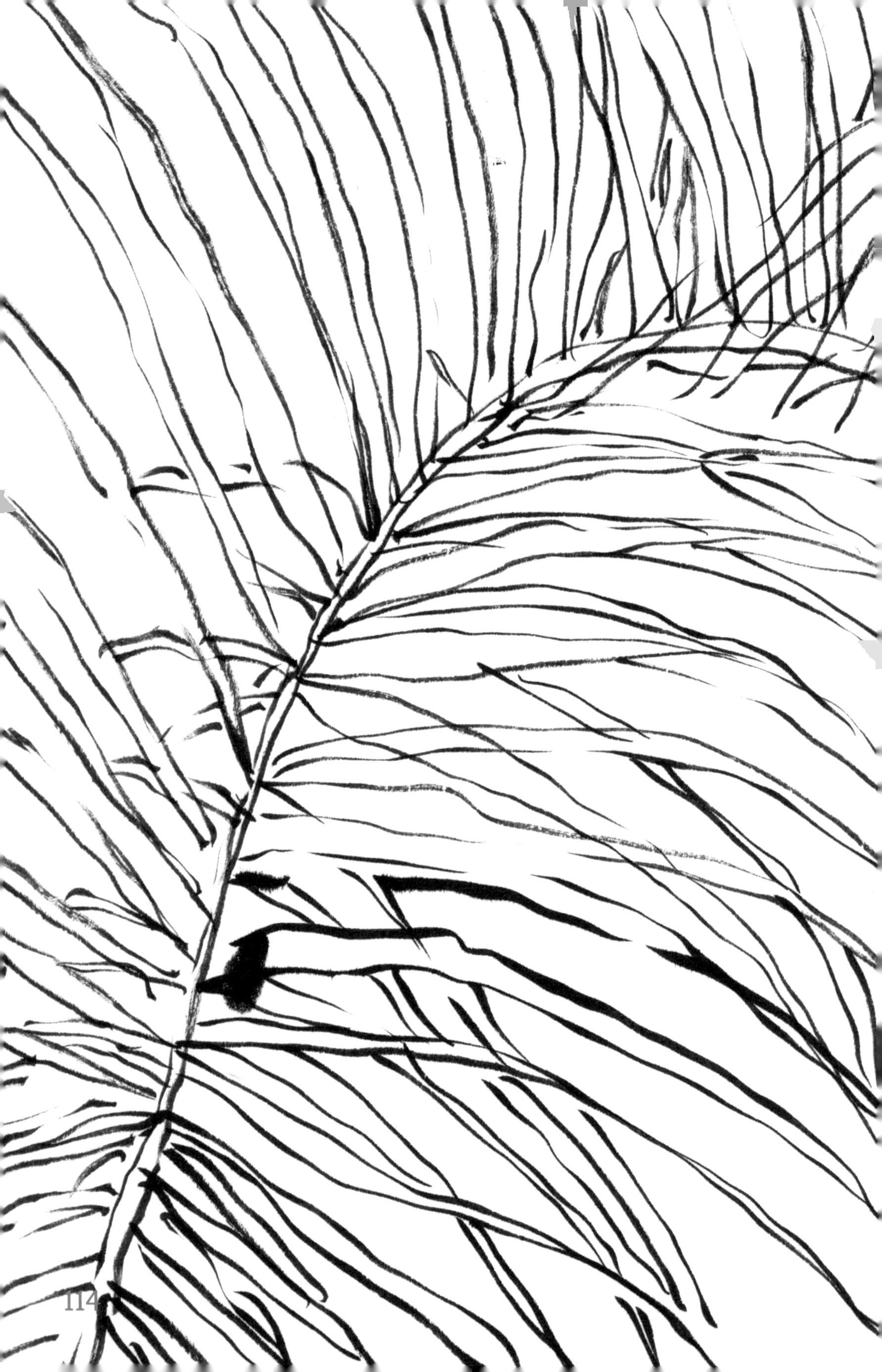

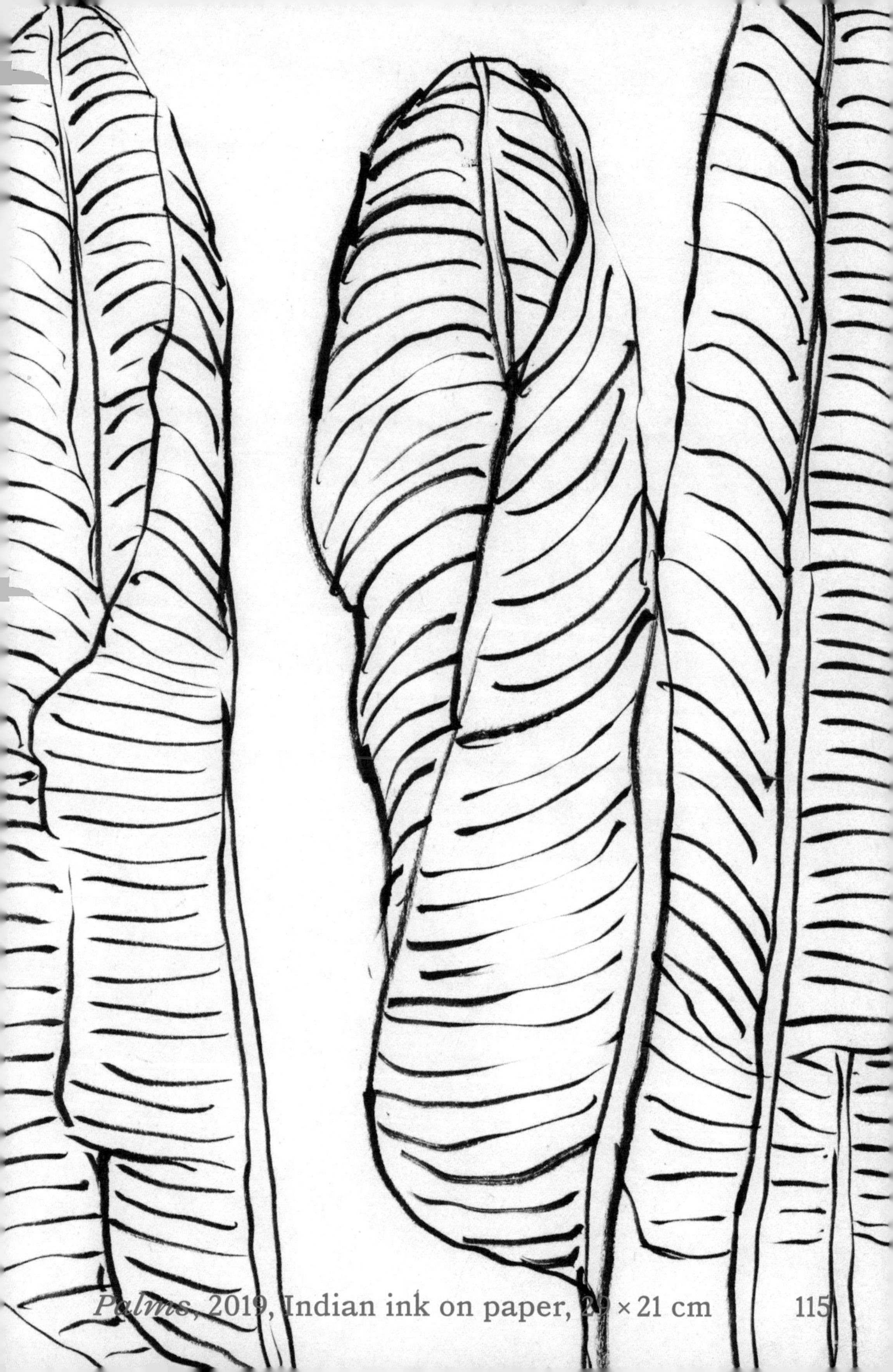

Palms, 2019, Indian ink on paper, 29 × 21 cm

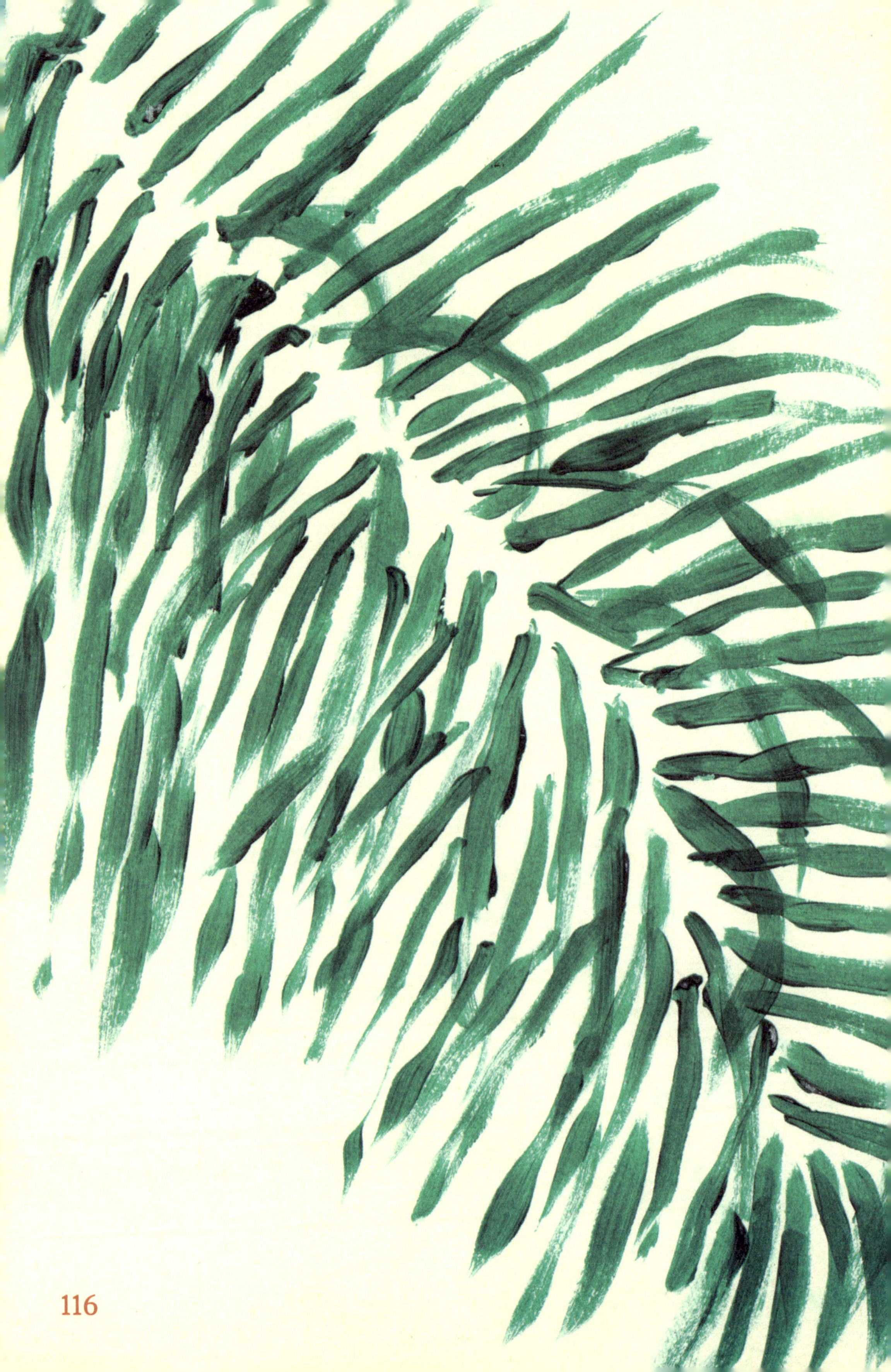

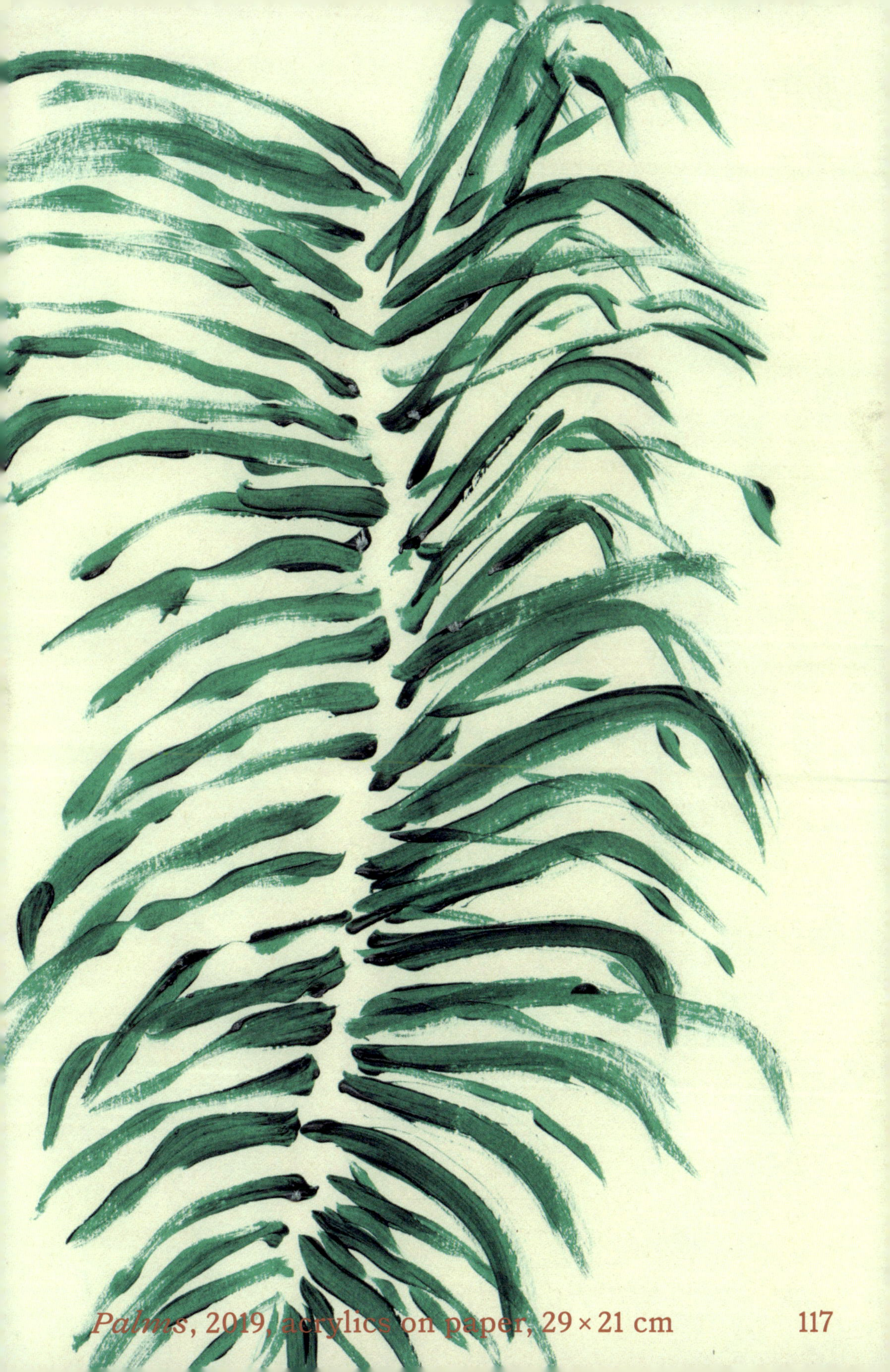

Palms, 2019, acrylics on paper, 29 × 21 cm

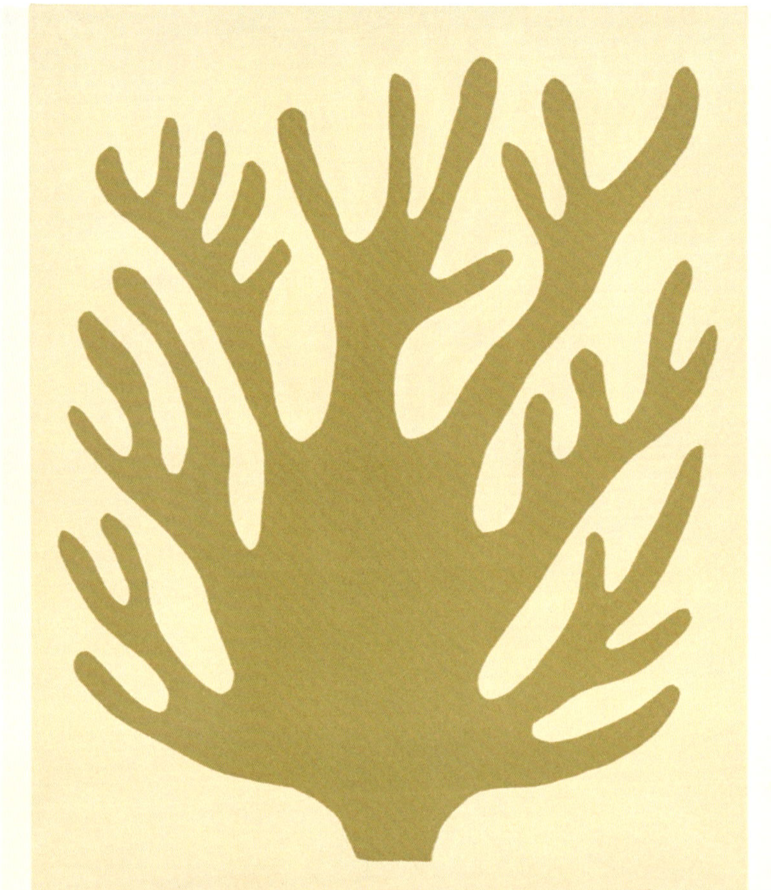

Ab Ovo. Green Alga, 2020, wool stitched on canvas, 104 × 86 cm

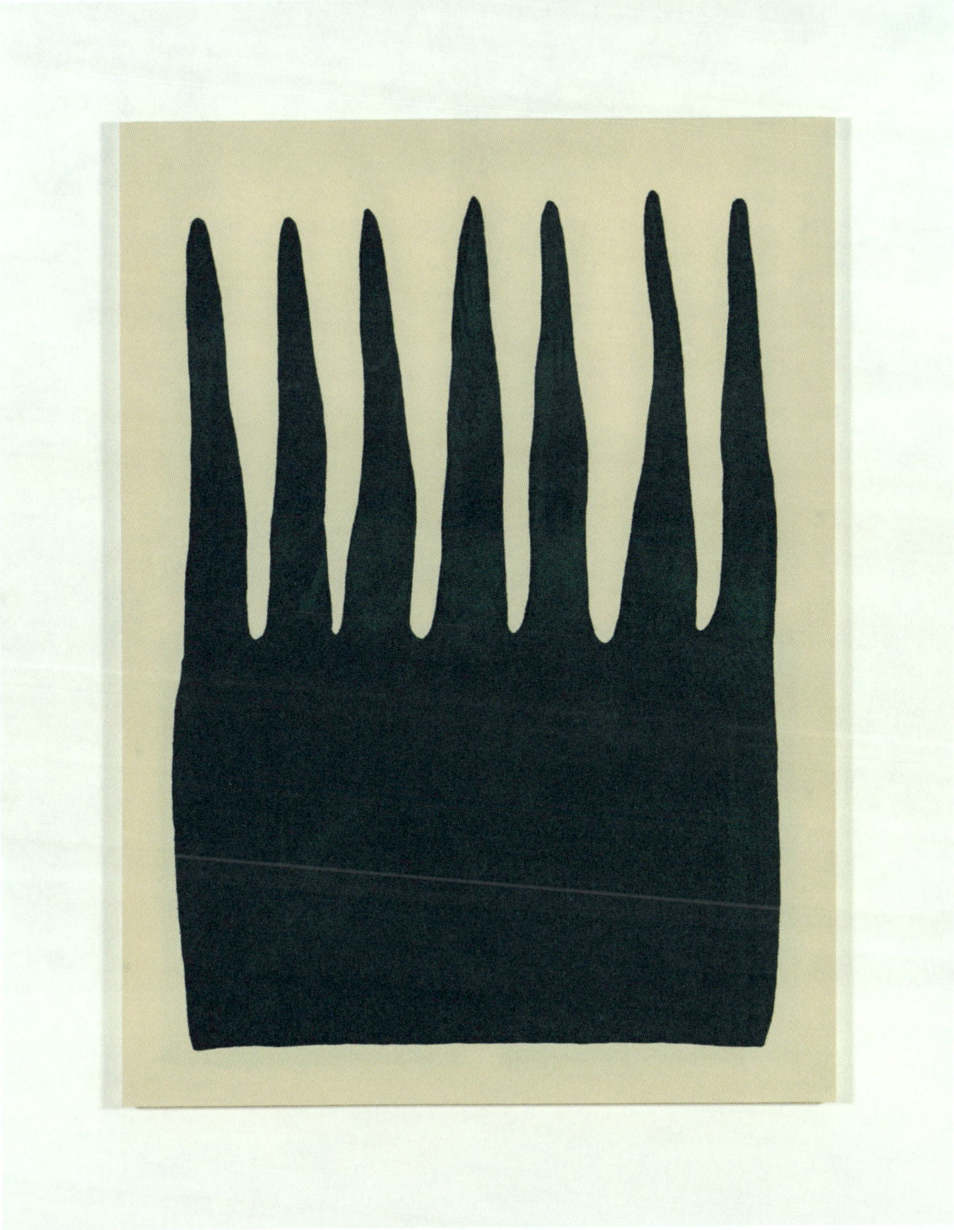

Ab Ovo. Green Palm, 2020, wool stitched on canvas, 158 × 118 cm

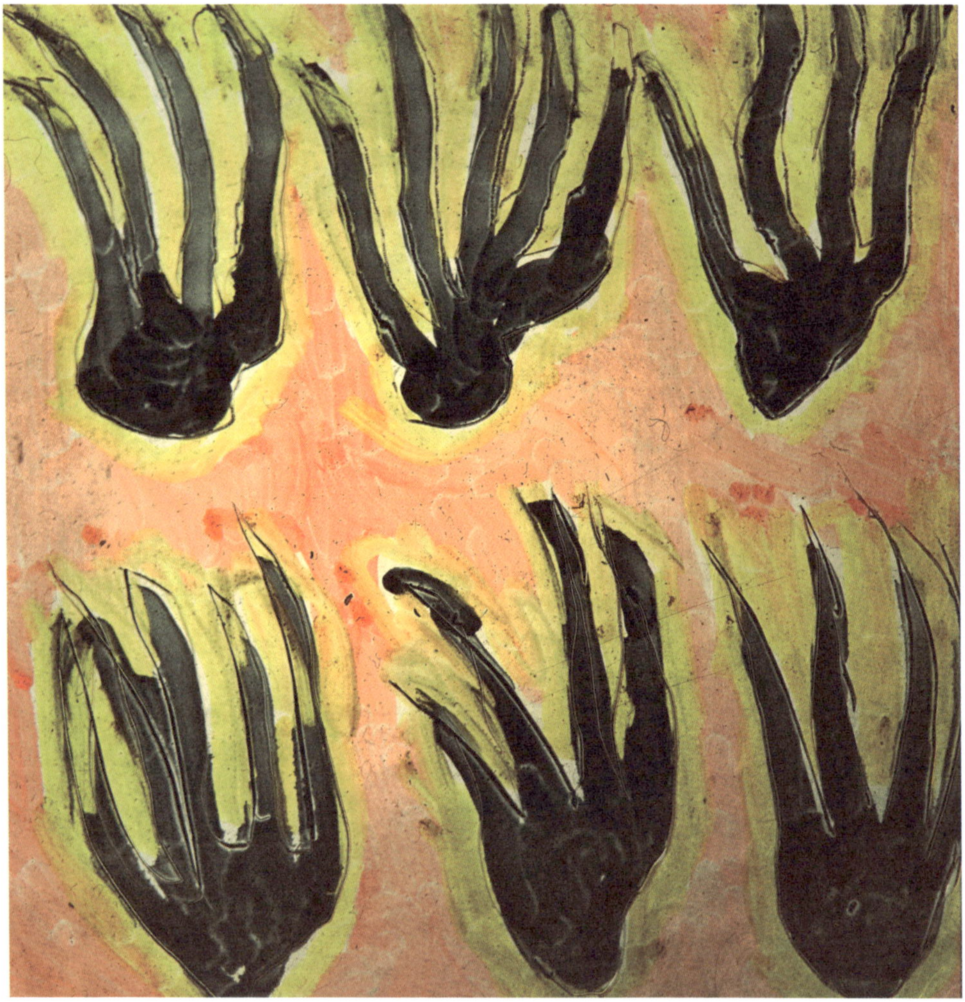

Ab Ovo. Field Notes, 2020, etching on diaposlide, Kodak Carousel projection

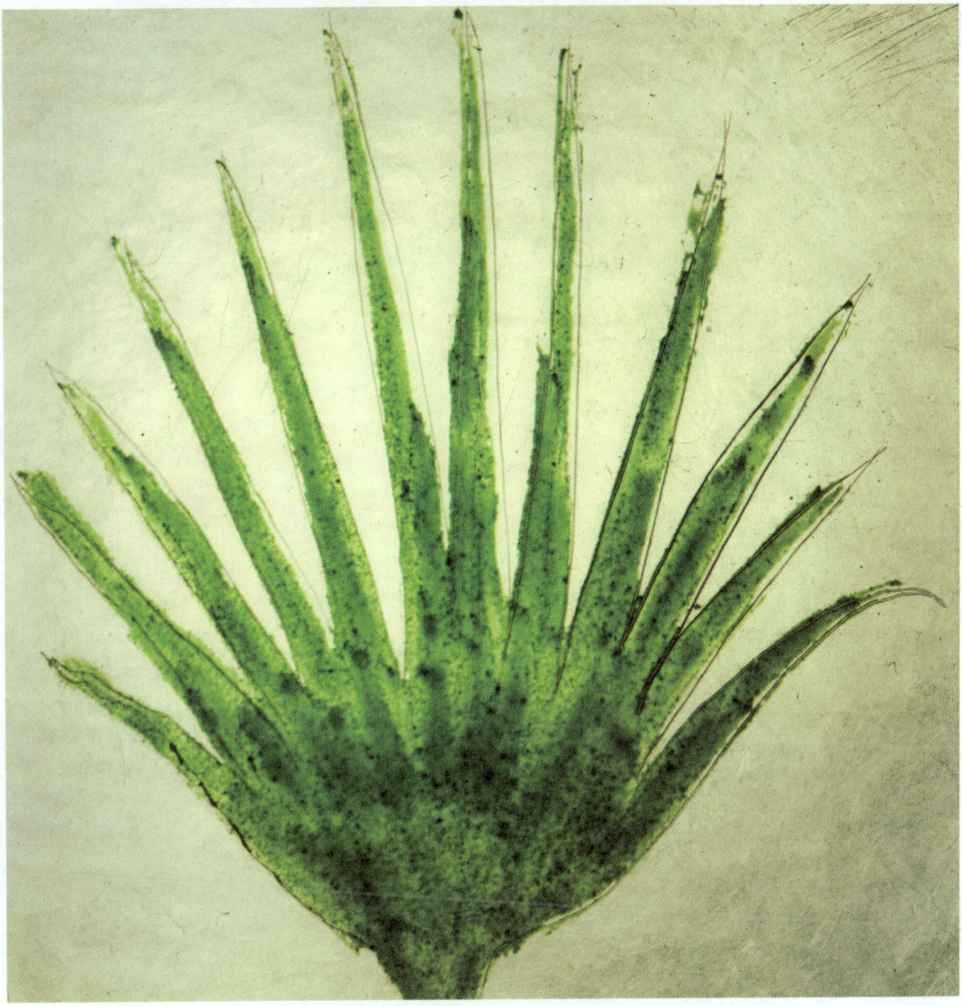

Ab Ovo. Field Notes, 2020, etching on diaposlide, Kodak Carousel projection

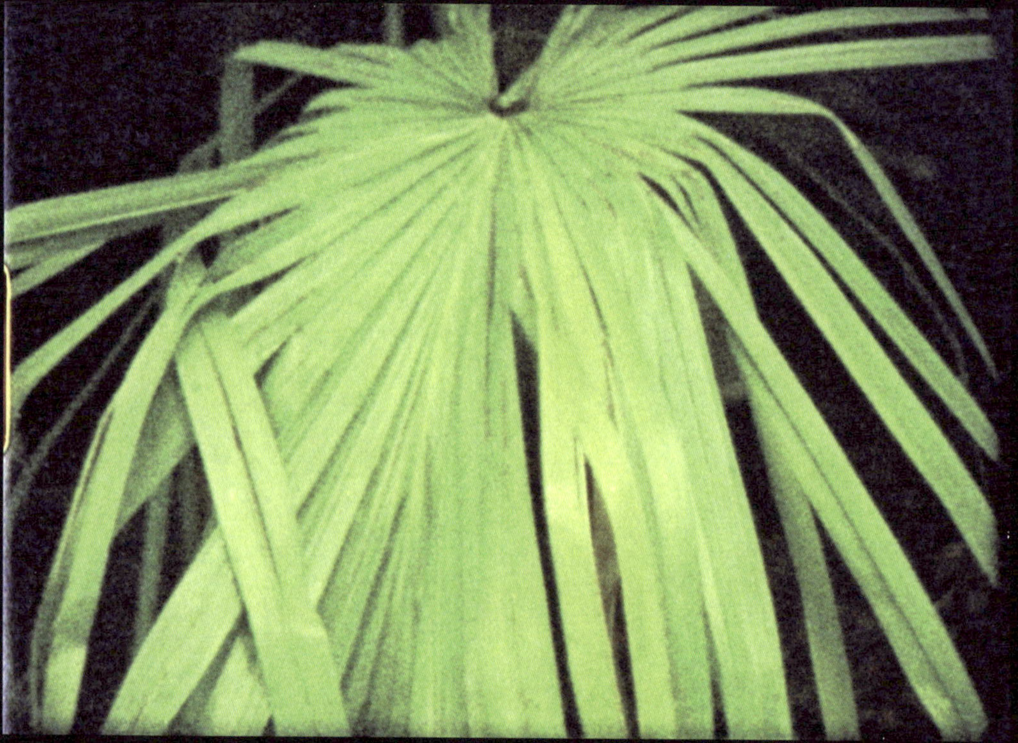

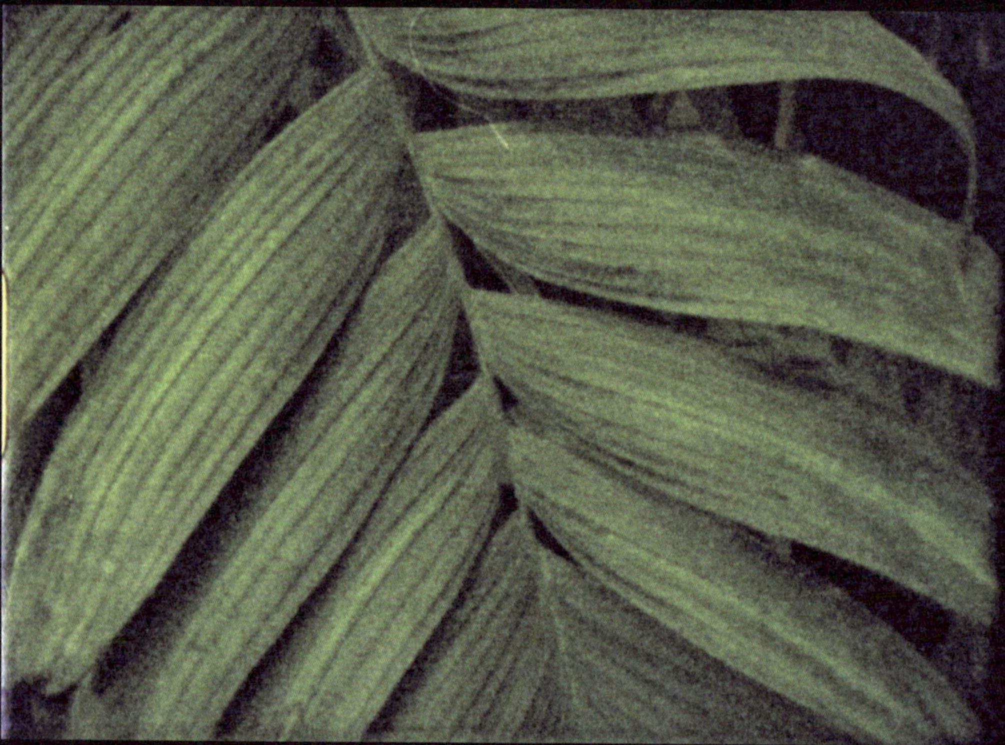

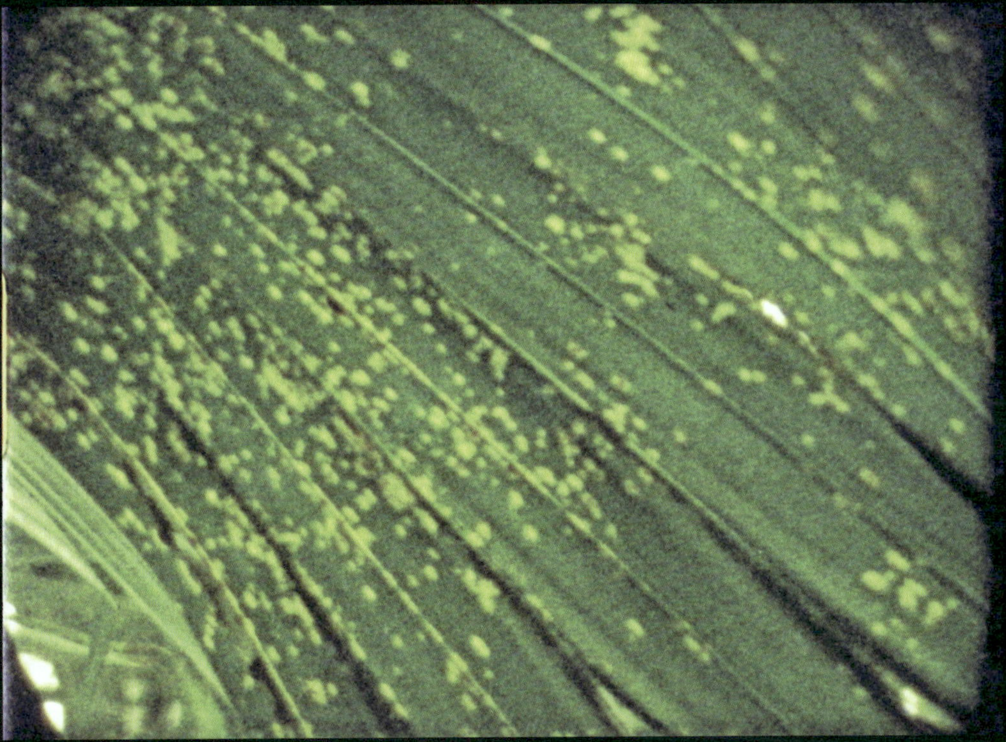

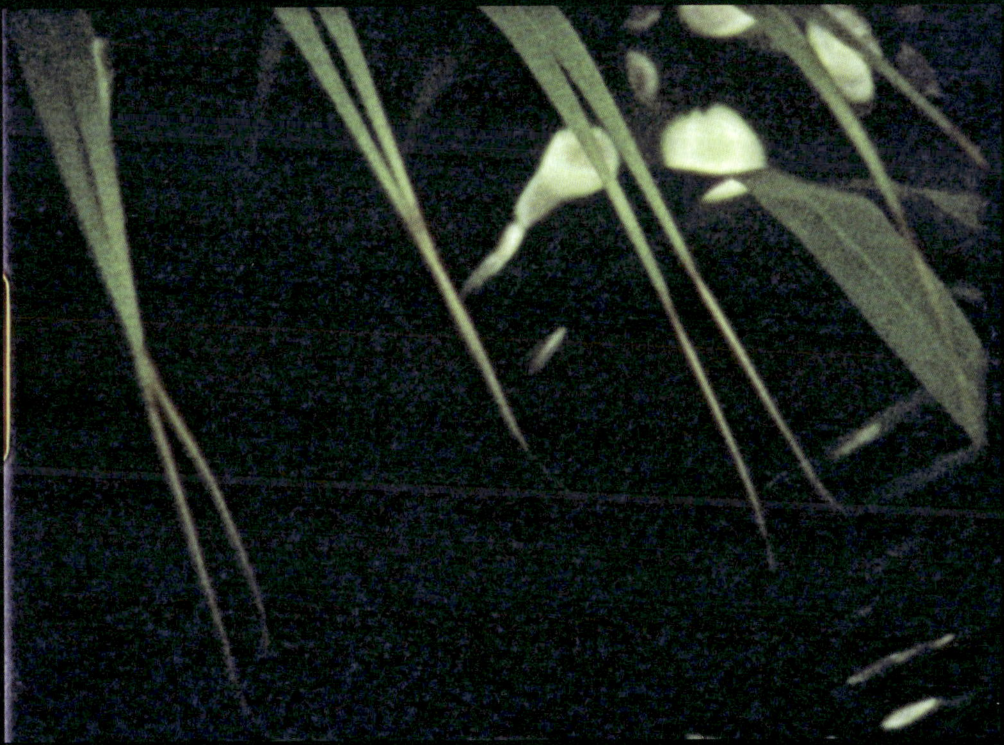

Stills from *Kew. A Conversation in Green*, 2019, super8 film, 3’09”

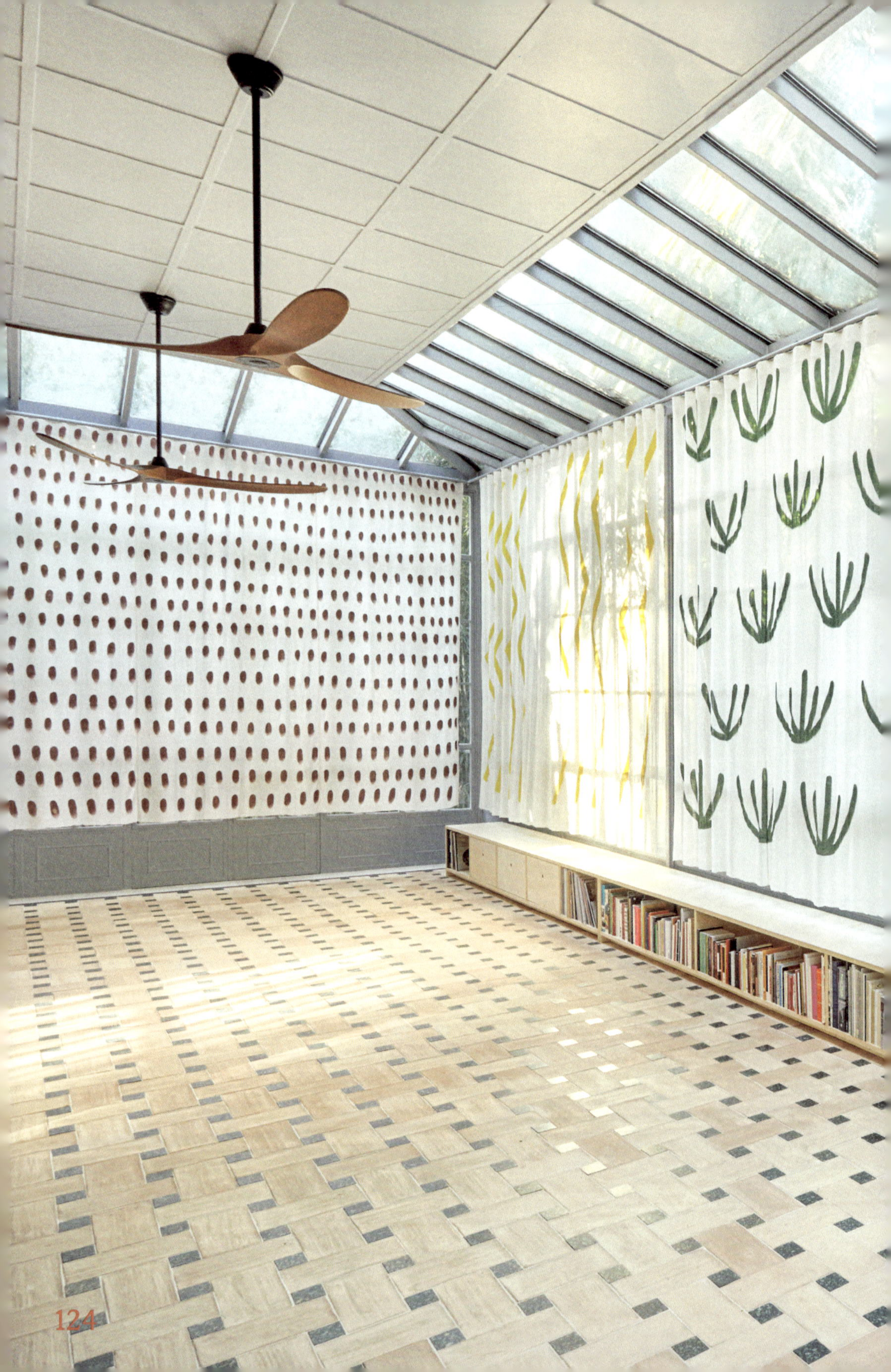

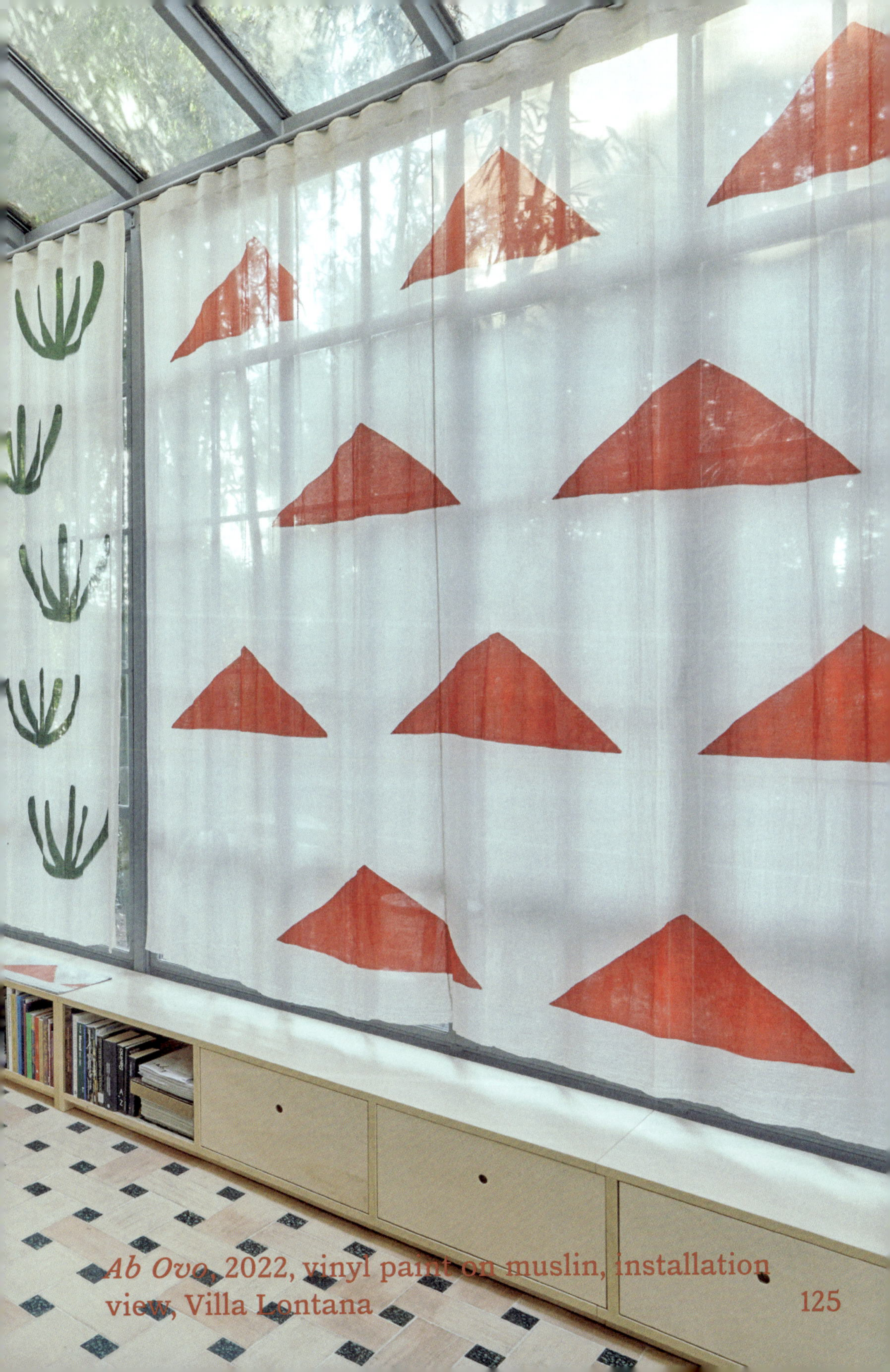

Ab Ovo, 2022, vinyl paint on muslin, installation view, Villa Lontana

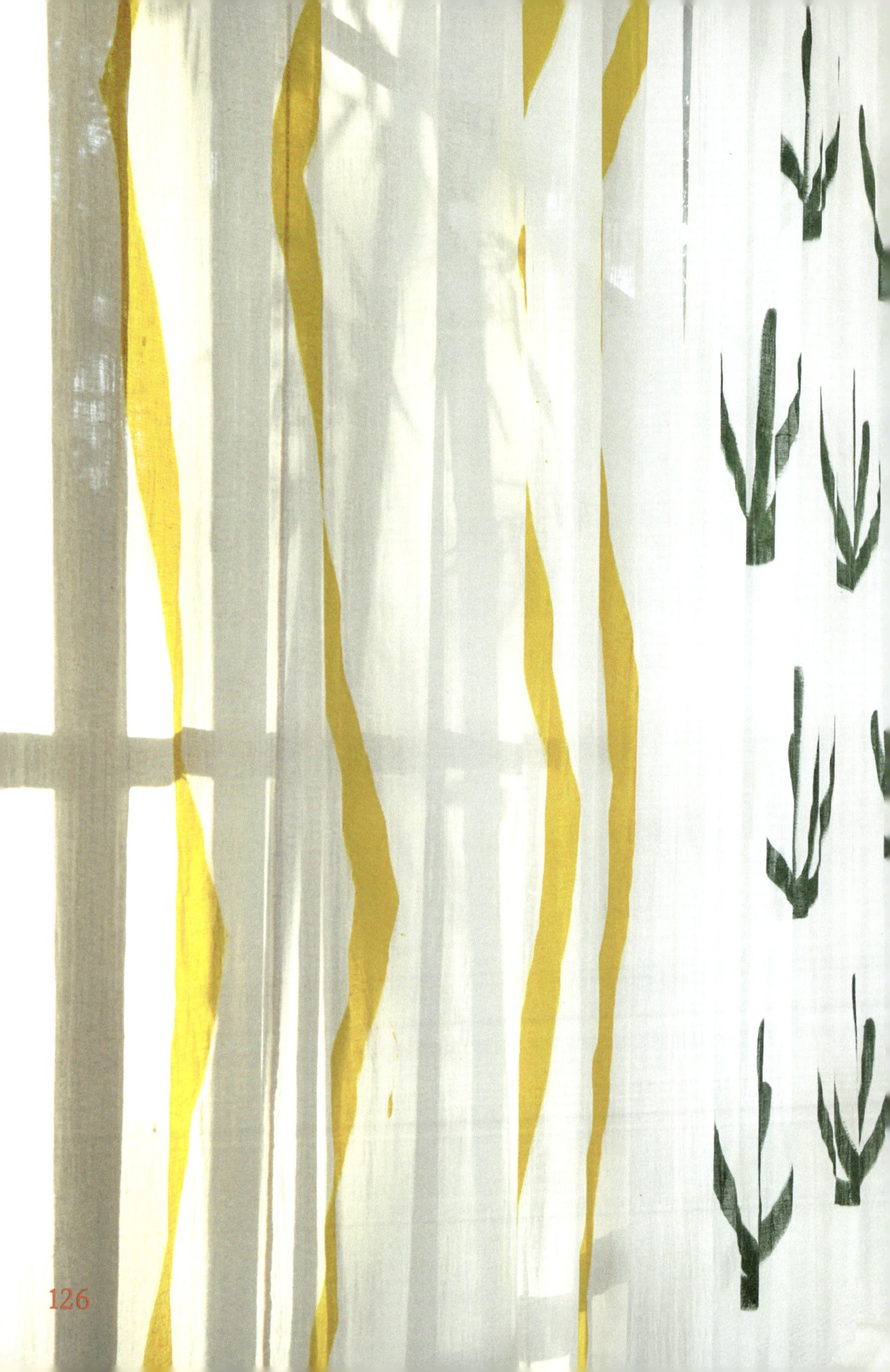

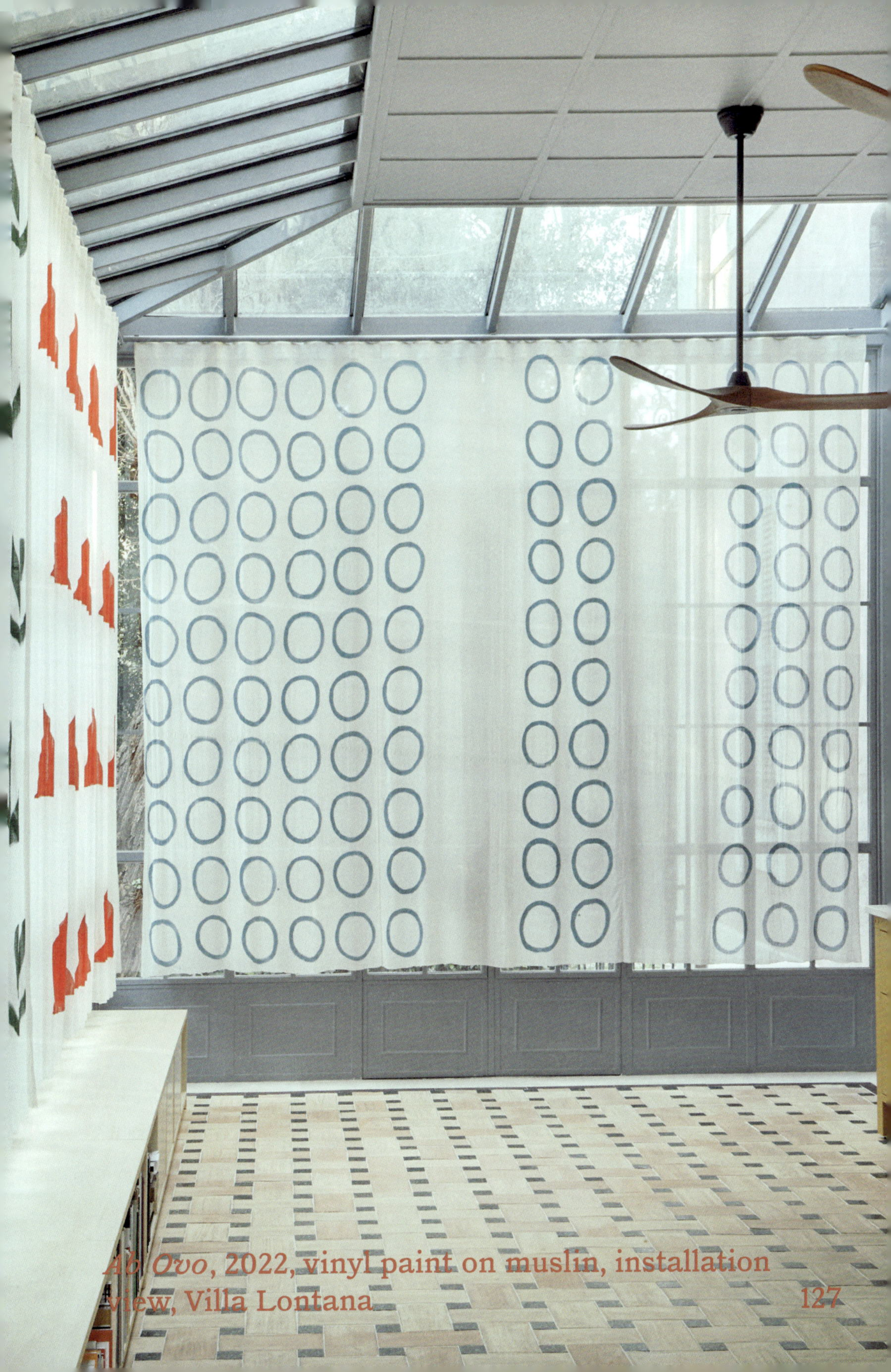

Ab Ovo, 2022, vinyl paint on muslin, installation view, Villa Lontana

I am interested in decoration because it virtually goes on forever, and yet it never narrates anything. So, what is it talking about? If I am not narrating anything, but I talk for hours, what am I saying?

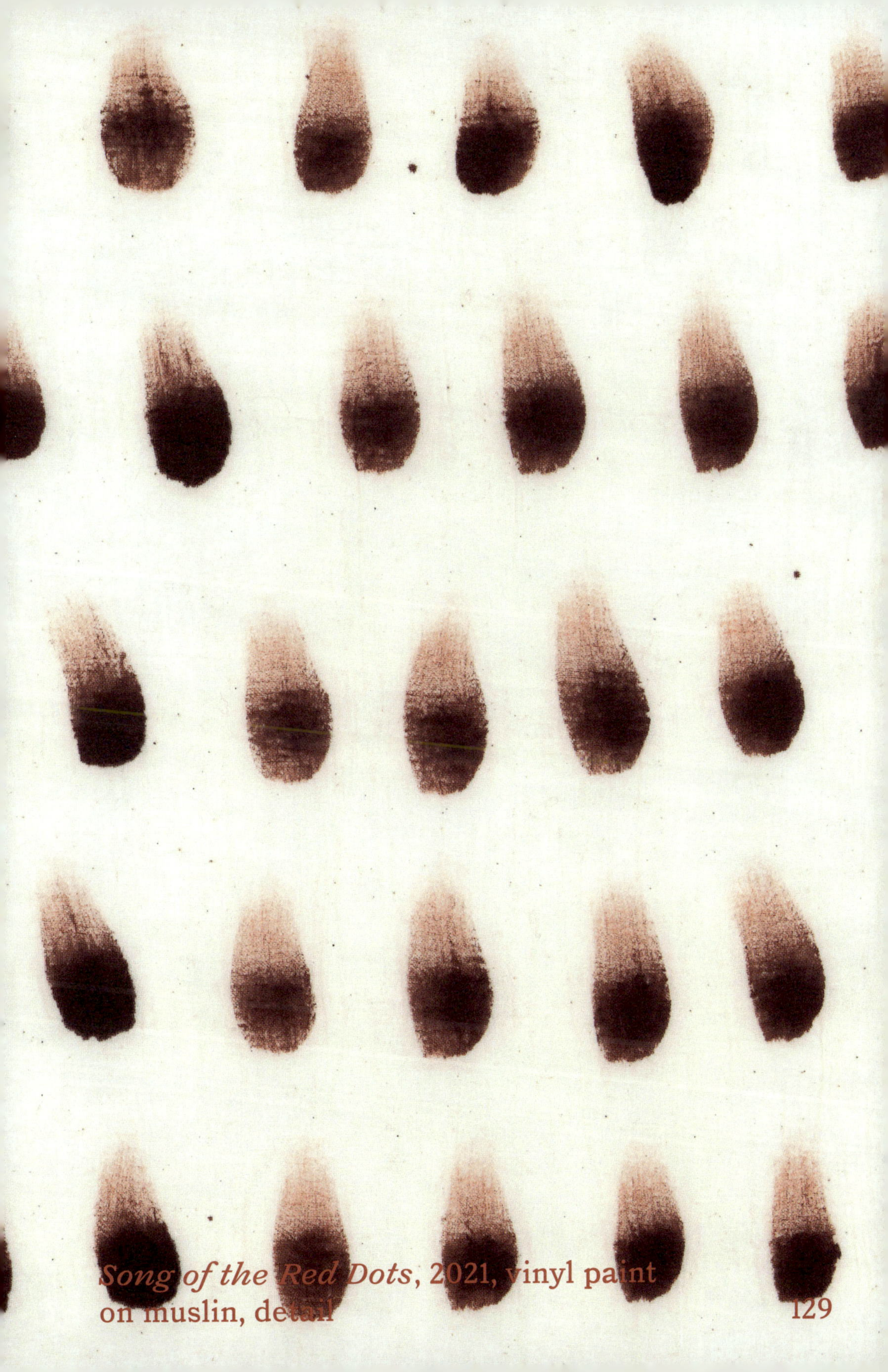

Song of the Red Dots, 2021, vinyl paint on muslin, detail

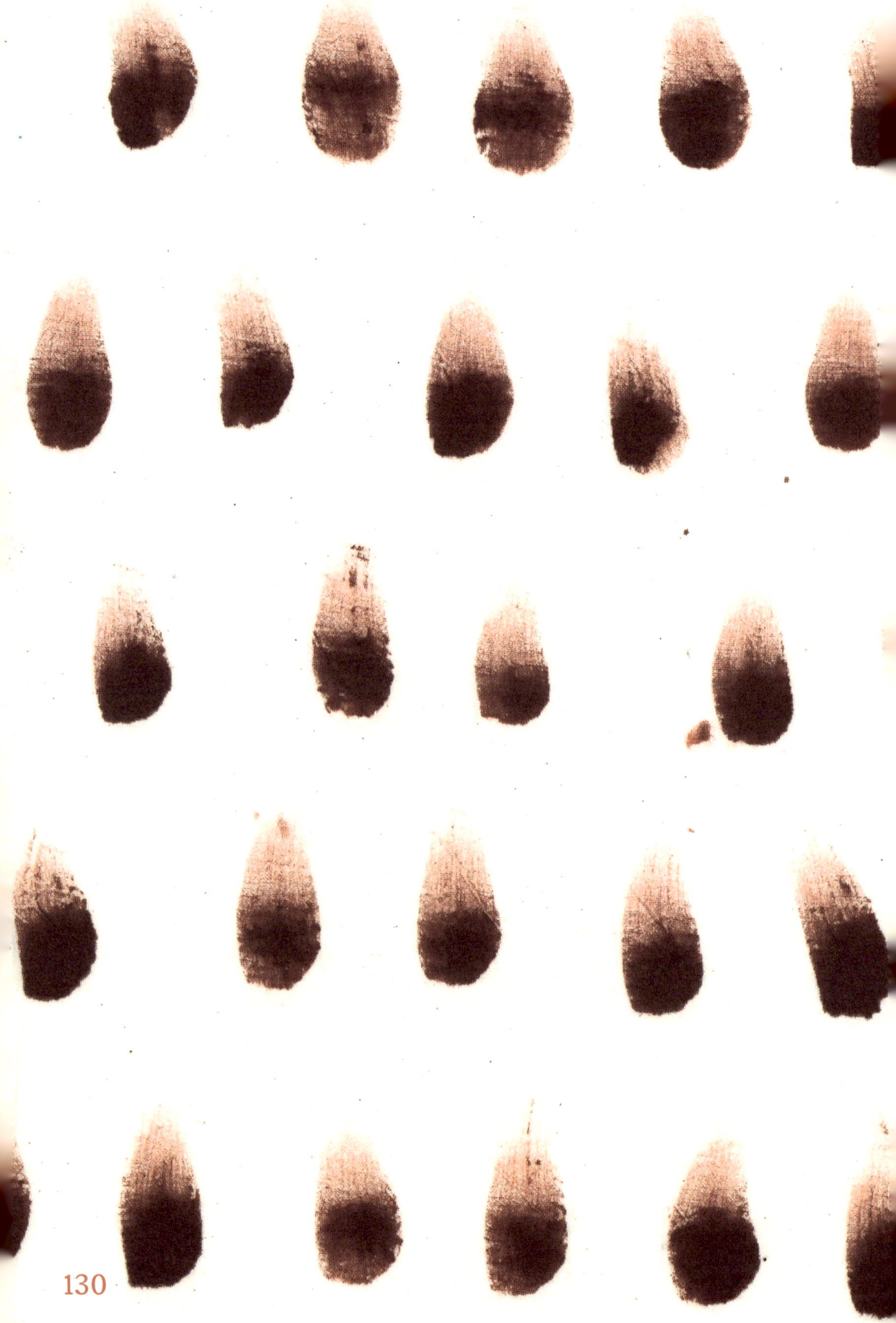

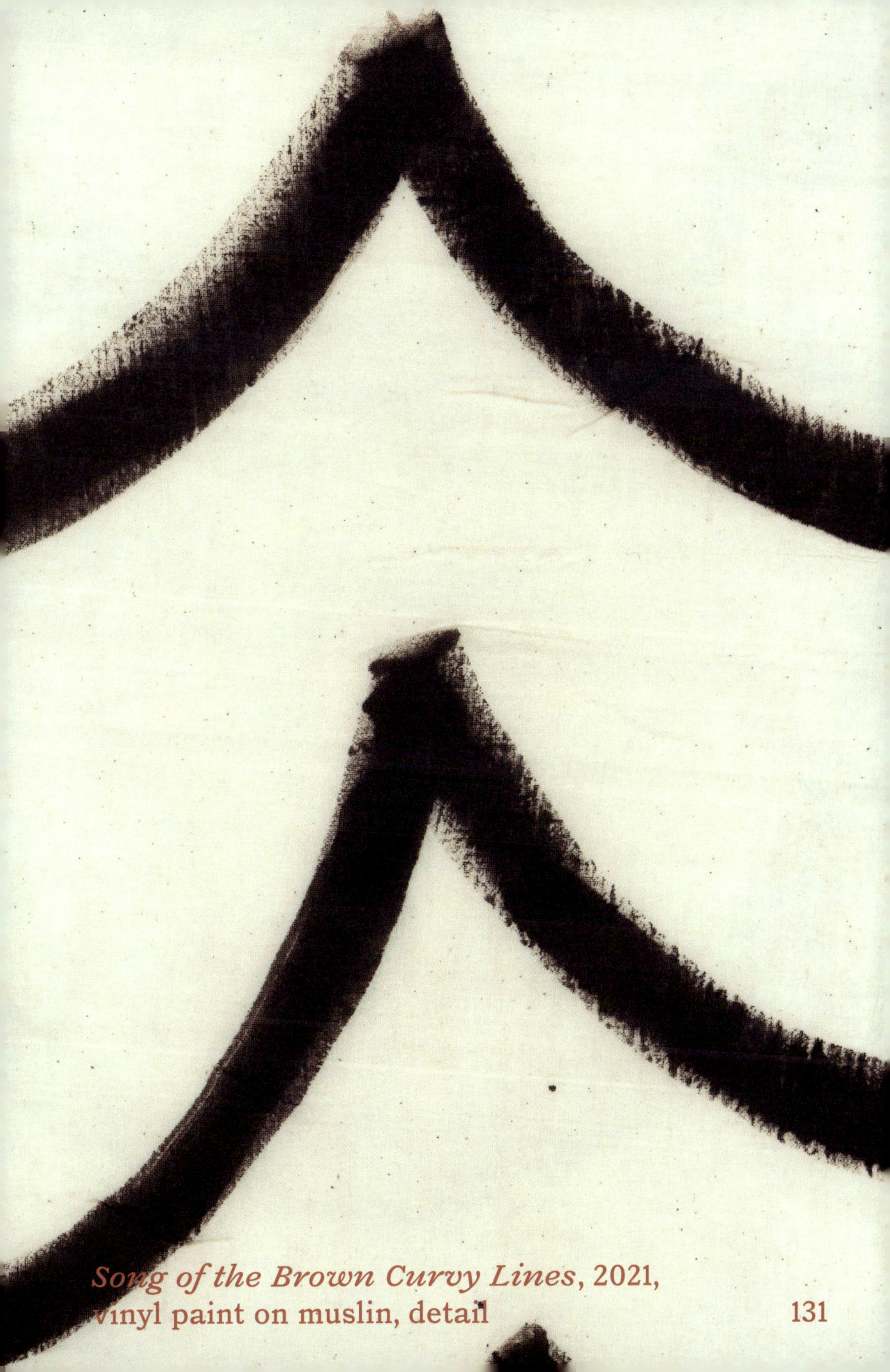

Song of the Brown Curvy Lines, 2021, vinyl paint on muslin, detail

Song of the Blue Lines, 2021, vinyl paint on muslin, detail

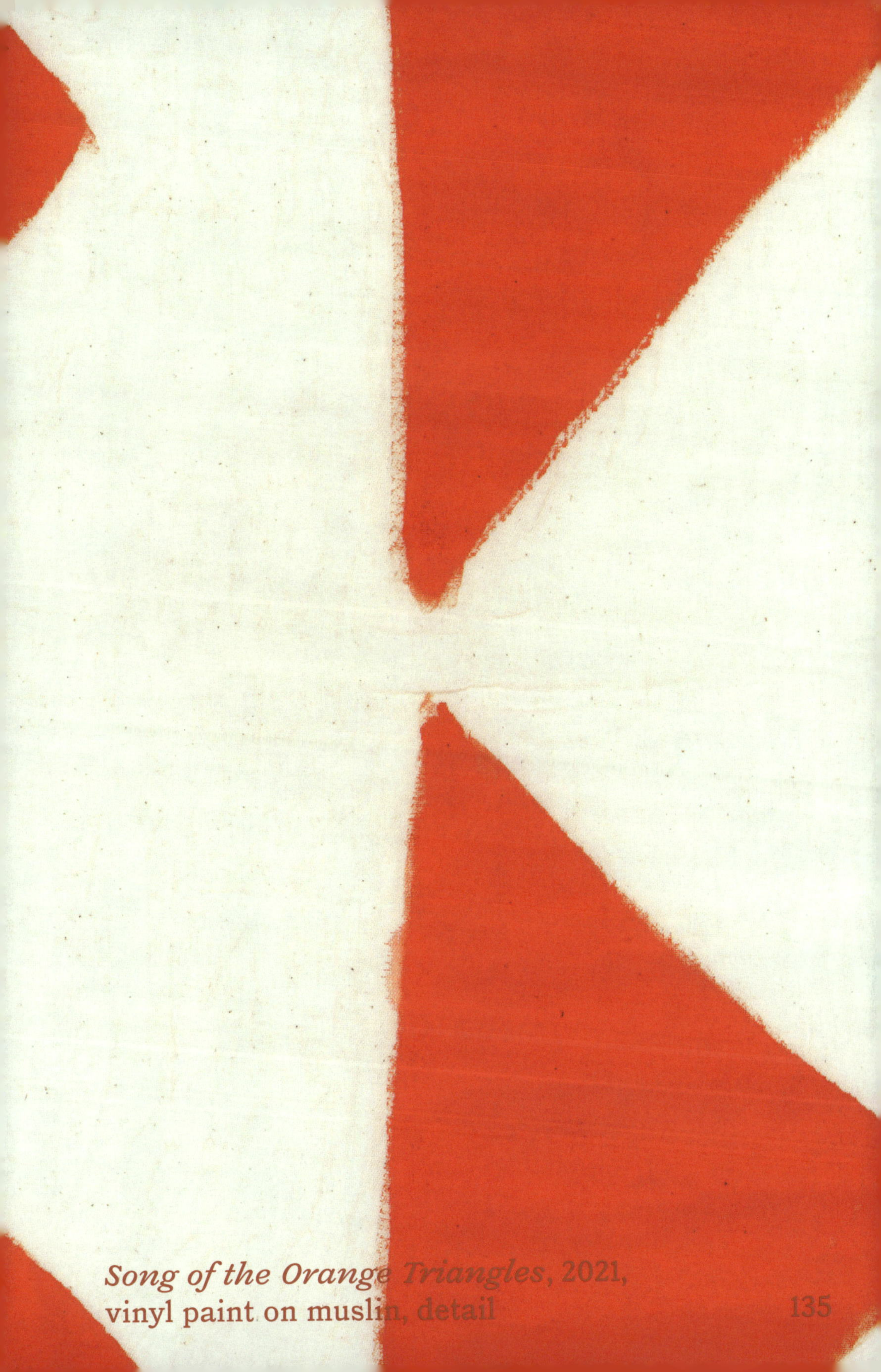

Song of the Orange Triangles, 2021, vinyl paint on muslin, detail

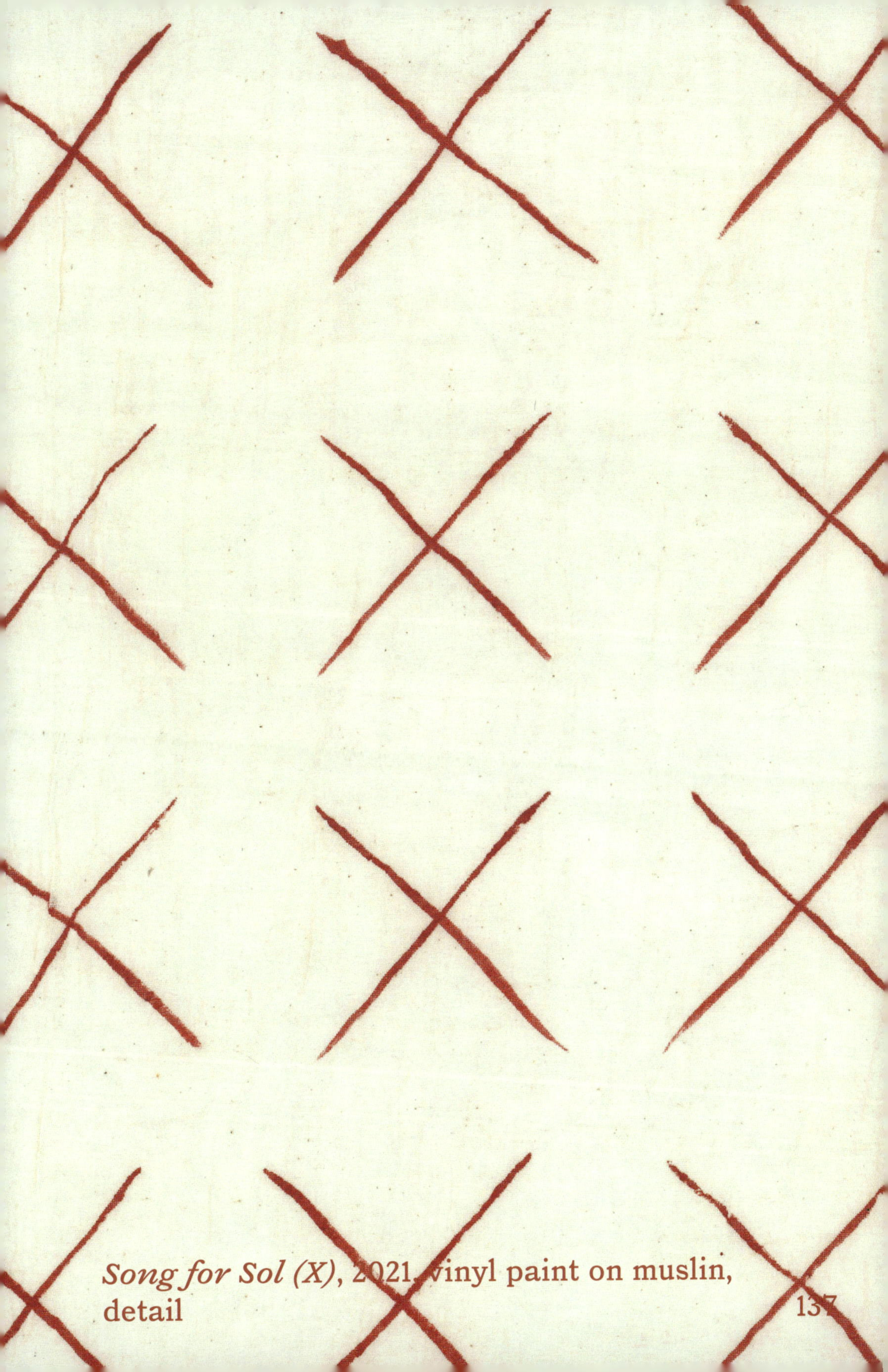

Song for Sol (X), 2021, vinyl paint on muslin, detail

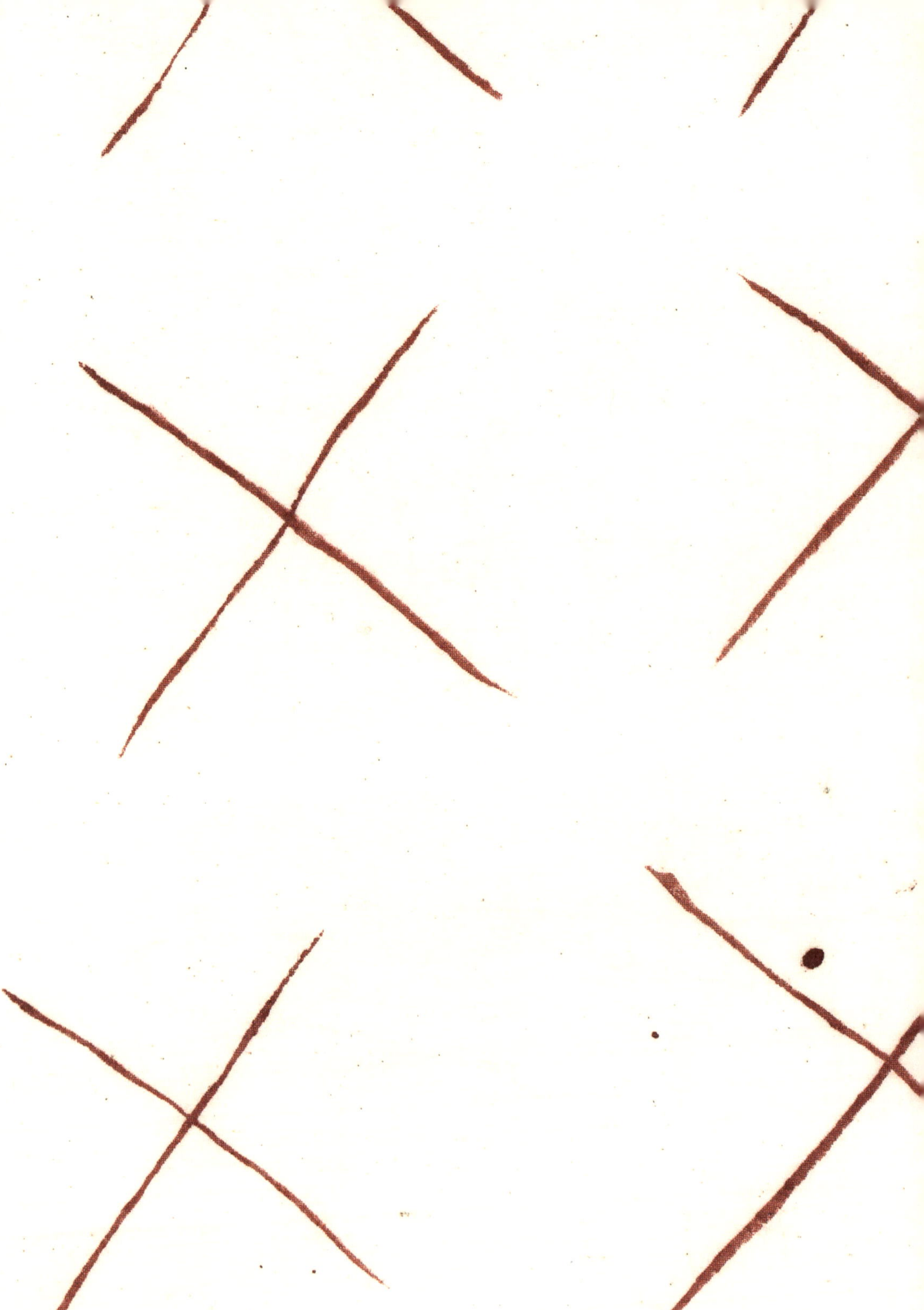

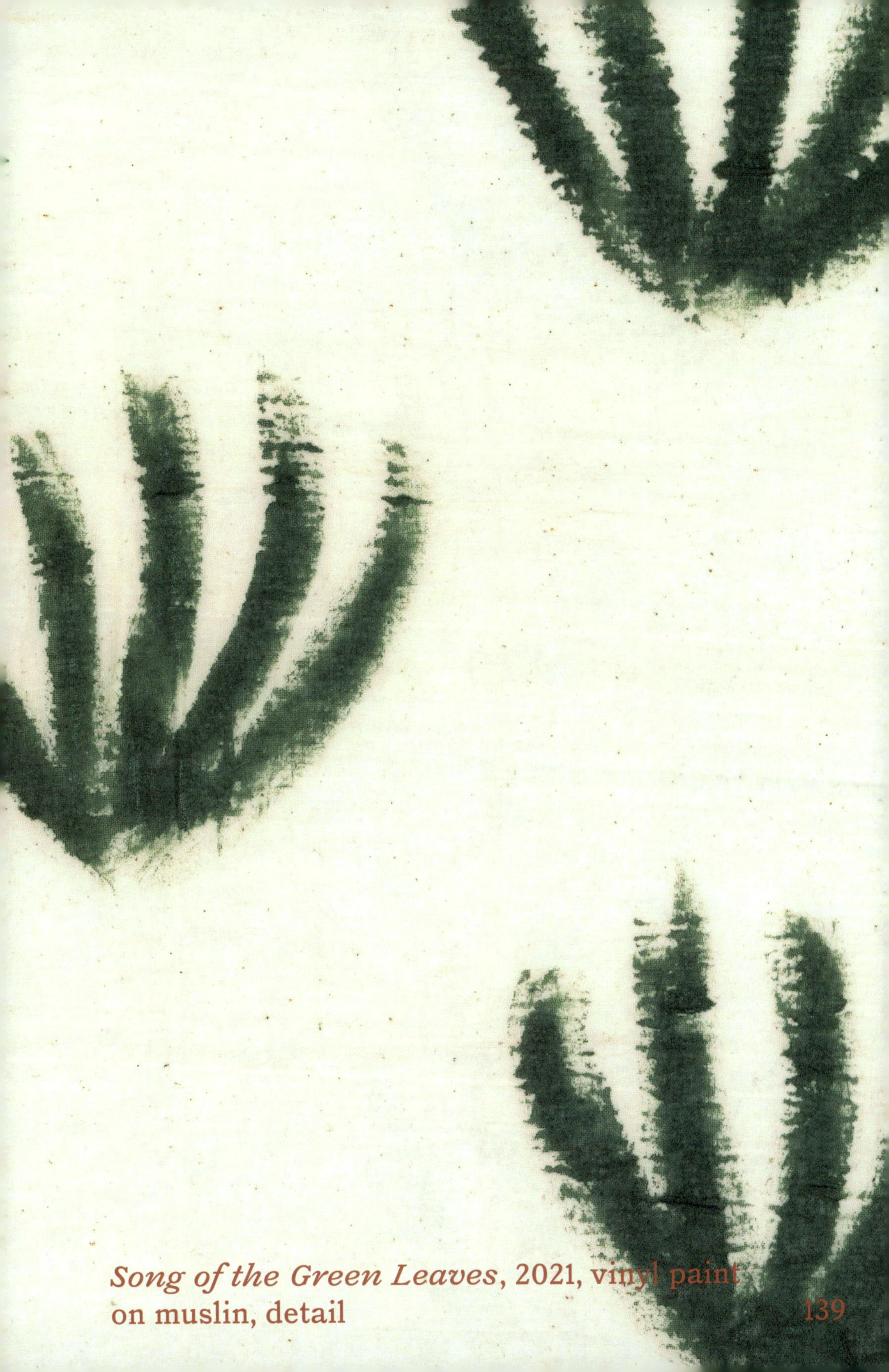

Song of the Green Leaves, 2021, vinyl paint on muslin, detail

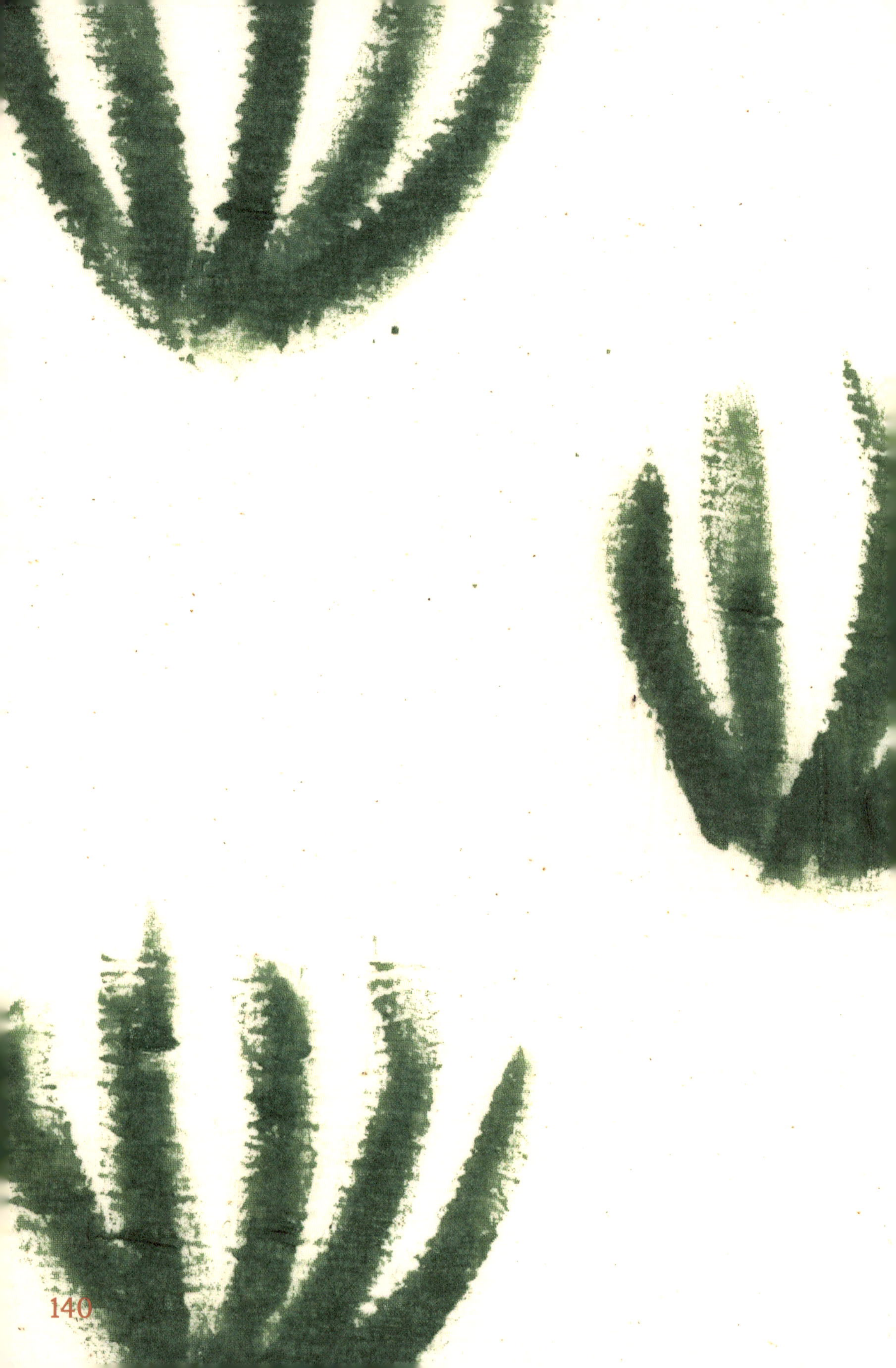

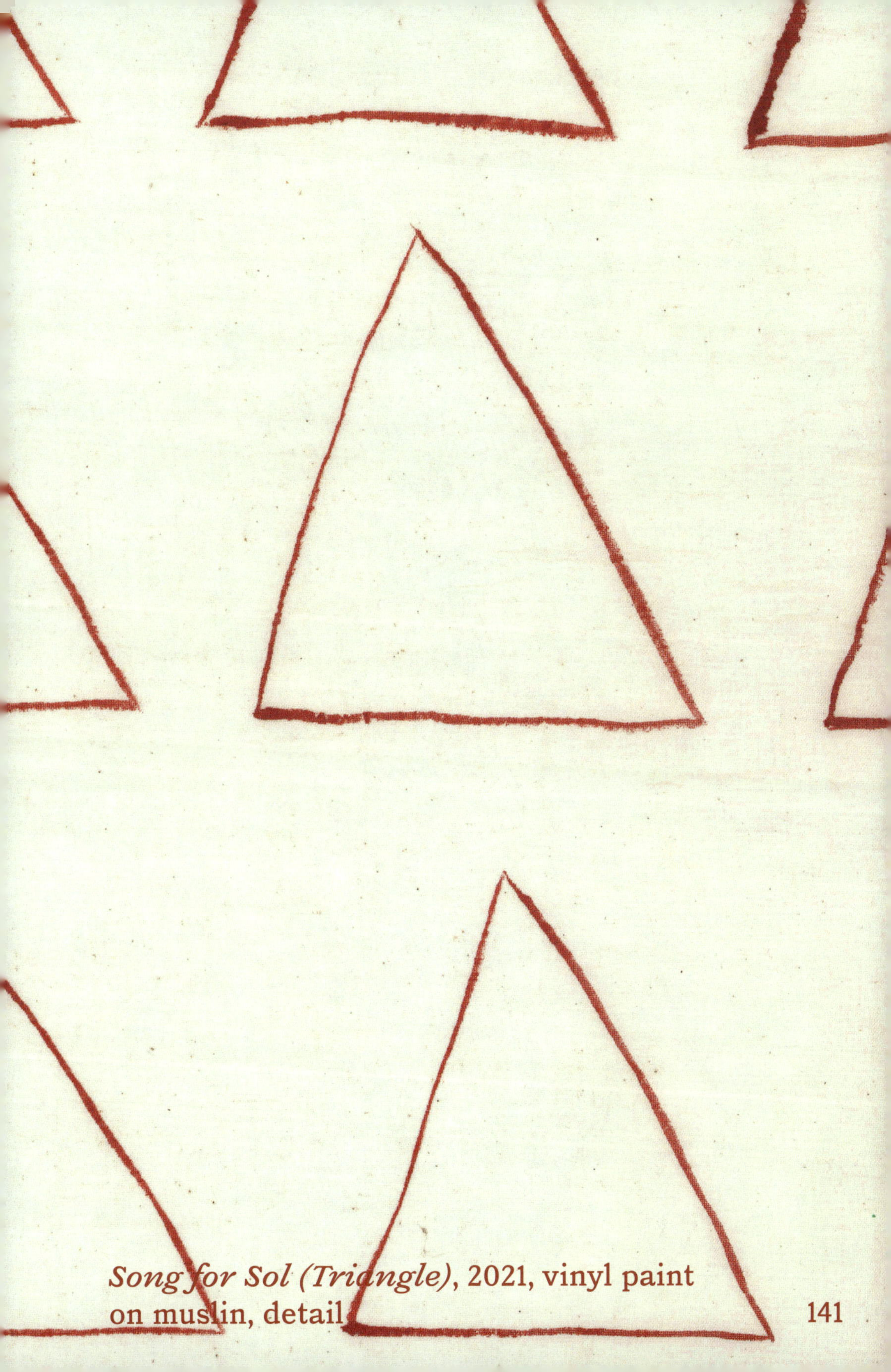

Song for Sol (Triangle), 2021, vinyl paint on muslin, detail

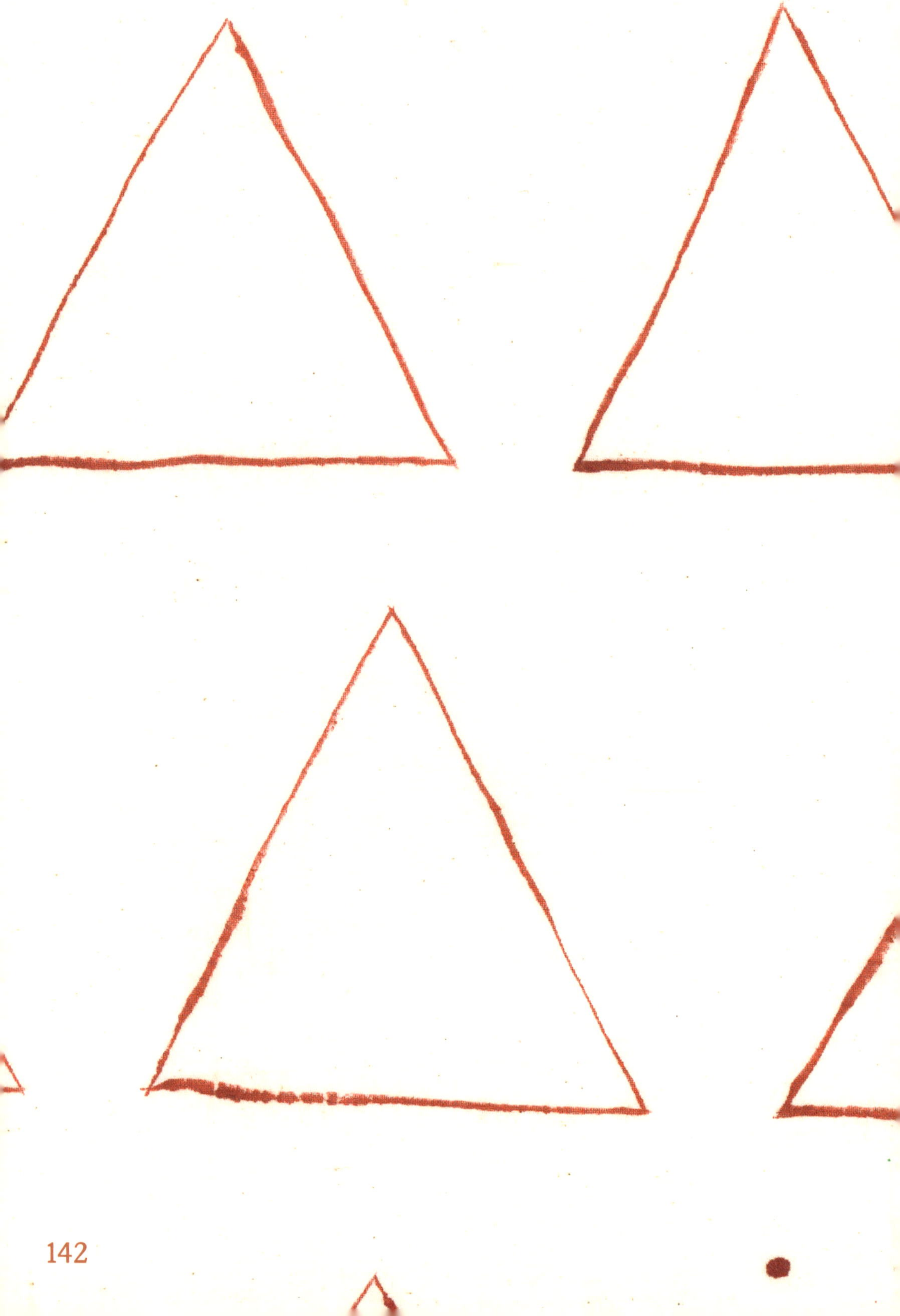

Acknowledgements

We are grateful to Emanuela Pigliacelli for her invaluable help along the project. This book would have never been possible without the steady encouragement of Fabiana Marenghi Vaselli Bond, Anna d'Amelio, Alessio Antoniolli, Daria Khan, Divya Osbon; and the rigour and creativity of the team at Mousse, Ilaria Bombelli, Alessandro Schino, Fiammetta Duke. Thanks to Fabrizio Padovani, Alessandro Pasotti, Chiara Tiberio and the whole team of P420, Bologna for their constant support. We would also like to thank Mistura Allison. We are grateful to the contributors to this publication, Jennifer Higgie, Jareh Das, Agnieszka Gratza, Cecilia Canziani. To Dom Bouffard, Temitope Ajose Cutting, Typhaine Delaup, Evie Hart for the collaboration on the performance. We would like to thank Efea Rutlin for her help. Finally, a special thanks to Guy Robertson and the Mahler & LeWitt Studios, where much of this work has started.

Photo Credits

p. 25 Claudio Oiticica, courtesy César and Claudio Oiticica
p. 42 Courtesy Victoria and Albert Museum, London
p. 49 2015, Agnes Martin / Artists Rights Society (ARS), New York
p. 66–71 Stephanie Black, courtesy the artist and P420, Bologna
p. 65, 72–85 Lewis Ronald, courtesy the artist and Mimosa House, London
p. 87, 91–98 Tim Smyth, courtesy the artist and Mimosa House, London
Cover, p. 13, 36, 48, 55, 102, 103, 106, 108, 110, 111, 113, 118–121 Carlo Favero, courtesy the artist and P420, Bologna
p. 124–127 Simon d'Exéa, site specific installation at Villa Lontana, Rome, commissioned by Vittoria Bonifati. Courtesy Fondazione Santarelli

Adelaide Cioni
On Patterns

Edited by Ilaria Puri Purini

First Published in 2023 on the occasion of the exhibition:
Adelaide Cioni
Ab Ovo / On Patterns
March 9th – April 25th, 2023
Mimosa House, London

Texts:
Cecilia Canziani
Jareh Das
Daria Khan
Agnieszka Gratza
Jennifer Higgie
Ilaria Puri Purini

Publishing Editor:
Ilaria Bombelli (Mousse)

Graphic Design:
Alessandro Schino (Mousse)

Translation:
Sylvia Adrian Notini

Proofreading:
Eleanor Margolies
Fiammetta Duke (Mousse)

Printed in Italy by:
Faenza Printing

Published and distributed by:
Mousse Publishing Contrappunto s.r.l.
via Pier Candido Decembrio 28,
20137, Milan–Italy

italianCouncil
Bringing our Contemporary Art to the World

MiC Direzione Generale Creatività Contemporanea

FONDAZIONE MEMMO GASWORKS

Mimosa House

Available through:

Mousse Publishing, Milan
moussemagazine.it
DAP | Distributed Art Publishers, New York
artbook.com
Les presses du réel, Dijon
lespressesdureel.com
Idea Books, Amsterdam
ideabooks.nl
Antenne Books, London
antennebooks.com

First edition
2023
ISBN 978-88-6749-576-4

€ 25 / $ 29.95

Project supported by Italian Council program (2022), promoted by the Directorate-General for Contemporary Creativity within the Italian Ministry of Culture.
In partnership with Fondazione Memmo, Rome and in collaboration with Gasworks, London.